IMAGES
of America

PEOPLE OF MIDDLESEX BOROUGH 1950–2008

Coming down the homestretch, the current members of the Middlesex Heritage Committee pore over the pictures that were gathered over the past year to make a final decision as to which should be included, why they should be featured, and where they should be placed in this book. Many enjoyable hours have been spent by the committee working at this dining room table to complete the publication of a second picture history of the borough.

On the cover: Pictured is the fourth-grade class of Pierce School posing for a picture during the 1958–1959 school year. These students are mostly members of the Middlesex High School class of 1967. To this day, they remain as close as they were during their high school years. Notice the focus in the faces of these young students, their appearance, and that of their classroom. (Courtesy of Middlesex Board of Education.)

IMAGES
of America

PEOPLE OF MIDDLESEX BOROUGH 1950–2008

Middlesex Borough Heritage Committee

ISBN 978-0-7385-6337-4

Published by Arcadia Publishing
Charleston SC, Chicago IL, Portsmouth NH, San Francisco CA

Printed in the United States of America

Library of Congress Catalog Card Number: 2008927311

For all general information contact Arcadia Publishing at:
Telephone 843-853-2070
Fax 843-853-0044
E-mail sales@arcadiapublishing.com
For customer service and orders:
Toll-Free 1-888-313-2665

Visit us on the Internet at www.arcadiapublishing.com

This book is dedicated to the memory of Jack Van Doren, former member of the Middlesex Borough Heritage Committee. Jack's enthusiasm, creativity, and courage added a special dimension to the committee's projects. Middlesex Borough remembers Jack with pride.

Contents

ACKNOWLEDGMENTS

Acknowledgment is given with thanks to the many photograph contributors. They include Dolores Ackerman, Nicholas Alimecco, Jane Andressen, Kathy Anthony, Lon Balunis, Diane Bank, James Benson, Mae Biondi, Anna Bitow, Ann Bodor, Joan Petty Boren, Ann Butera, Bob and Cathy Canavan, Peter Ciliberto, Tracey Coble, Bette Comune, Jim and Sandy Creighton, Frank and Jack DeAngelis, Delta Cleaners, Oreste "Rusty" DeSiato, Kate Diskin, Mary Diskin, Ronald and Blanche Dobies, Kevin Dotey, Walter and Phyllis Durniak, Myra Efinger, John Ellery, Jennifer Emrich, Bart Fellin, James Fiorentino, Steve Fisk, Greg Freeman, John and Sheila Fuhrmann, Mary Ann Gazi, Niki Gerondelis, Barbara Gorman, Bob Green, Harold Green, Joe and Teri Hoski, James Hower, Michael Jesionka, Nancy Johnson, Tim and Betsy Kerwin, Kathryn Kinstler, Carol Kirk, Michael Kozik, Nick Lance, Eileen Liming, Phil and Rita Lopa, Jeff Maree, Patricia Martin, Bud Mastrull, Anne Matuskiewicz, Steve Mavrionis family, Middlesex Borough Rescue Squad, Middlesex Borough Schools, Kay Mulrooney, Elsie Nelson family, Our Lady of Mount Virgin School, Rich Pachucki, Margaret Paradis, Sherley Penrose, Lossie Pitt, Dave and Debbie Polakiowicz, Paige Price, Jake Qiku, Eleanor Rajca, Michael Renda, Lyn Rinker, Claire Ritchie, Ray Romano, Richard Rutkowski, Walter Ryan, Marie Sabecky, Angiolina Sansone, Monique and Tony Sasso, Georgianna Schaub-Snyder, Judy Schoenrock, Norman Seip, Theresa Senna, Bob and Sylvia Sobotka, Edythe Staffelli, Maureen Tagliaferro, George and Vicki Vuolde, Joe and Agnes Waide, Rosemary Walsh, Scott Walsh, Mary Watese, Beverly Weber, Charlie Weis, Ed Winters, William Yudicki, and Joseph Zuccarelli.

—Middlesex Borough Heritage Committee
Peter Diskin
Catherine Ferris
Robert Ferris
Edward J. Johnson Jr.
Mary L. Johnson
Alex Morecraft
Peter Staffelli

INTRODUCTION

Middlesex Borough, at the midpoint of the 20th century, was a relatively undeveloped town. In 1950, there was no shopping center, no bank, no library, and no high school. Route 28 was a two-lane road with many open fields on both sides. There were many open areas throughout the borough. Teenagers had many choices in which to choose up sides and play sandlot baseball, softball, football, or a variety of other self-created and nonorganized athletic activities and games with friends.

At that time, neighboring Bound Brook was the center of activity for most Middlesex residents. Teenagers walked two miles back and forth to Bound Brook High School and utilized the Bound Brook Library for reading and research. Most town residents used the Bound Brook shopping area and had to go out of town for medical, dental, and pharmacy services.

In 1950, Middlesex was a town of four square miles with a census total of 5,947 and an average of 1,850 people per square mile. The 1980 population was 13,480. Population in the year 2000 was 13,717, an increase of only 237 people over a 20-year period. The post–World War II period between 1946 and 1970 showed rapid increases in property development and town population, while after 1970, housing development was more limited with very stable population totals.

Louis Staffelli was the mayor during the immediate years after World War II, serving until 1954. There was a building boom of single-family houses after the war, as was evidenced by the construction of Watchung Estates during his tenure. A land freeze during that era created much open area and resulted in checked and coordinated real estate development. Other areas developed were the Homestead sections near Dunellen, Foothill Acres, Creighton Manor, and the extension of Beechwood Avenue.

During the 1950s, there were over 150 small businesses and manufacturing establishments in the borough, representing a wide variety of industrial interests. Also present were 11 greenhouses, including the world's largest producer of orchids. The greenhouses provided job opportunities for local residents throughout the years. Family ownership of the greenhouses through the generations from father to son is evidenced today by the floral business operations of the Biondi, Boehme, and Ferris families. The Hoski family business is also another example of a long-established florist in the community. Once known as "Flowertown USA," Middlesex marked its 50th anniversary as a town of its own with the Flowertown parade in 1963.

The Parker, Pierce, and Watchung public schools existed in 1950, enjoying long histories of instruction for Middlesex students. Central School was completed in 1954 under the leadership of the beloved superintendent of schools Von E. Mauger, in whose honor the school was renamed in 1975. An addition to the Von E. Mauger School began in 1998 and was completed in 2000.

The parochial school, Our Lady of Mount Virgin, opened its doors in 1955 and was built by future mayor Walter L. Rafferty. Educational and community leaders worked closely together doing all the preliminary work to begin construction of Middlesex High School in 1957. The school was completed and opened in 1959. The class of 1962 was the first graduating class, and an addition to the high school was completed in 1970. Hazelwood School opened its doors for kindergarten through fifth grade in 1966. Pierce School was closed in 1983 and demolished in 1984.

In 1949, Staffelli appointed a recreation committee to plan a yearlong recreation program that led to the formation of the first recreation commission in the early 1950s. At that time, Victor Crowell Park was the only park owned and operated by the borough. Today Middlesex offers an outstanding park system and recreational programs, as evidenced by the recent beautification program at Victor Crowell Park, the facilities at Mountainview Park, Worowski Field, Haverstick Park, Simchock Field, Charles Morgan Memorial Field, and the Little League ballpark.

The Roy Harkness Community Pool has been in operation since 1966. It was named for the chairman of the original swim pool committee. The community pool offers not only summer leisure but also a variety of swimming lessons and other pool-related programs.

Intellectual pursuits may be attained at the Middlesex Public Library. Established in 1962, the town library was opened in 1963 in a storefront building on Bound Brook Road and housed only 100 reference books. In 1964, the library moved to an old building in Mountainview Park. Groundbreaking ceremonies for the present library located on Mountain Avenue began in 1969 and construction was completed in 1970. A large addition to the library was completed in 2002.

Health, safety, and security are paramount in the minds and hearts of community citizens for themselves, their families, and their properties. These services are provided by the Middlesex Board of Health, the Middlesex Borough Rescue Squad, the office of emergency management, the borough's office for the aging, the Middlesex Police Department, and the Middlesex Fire Department.

The Middlesex Fire Department celebrated its 100th anniversary in 2005, based on the fact that the Lincoln Hose Company was in existence in 1905. The Beechwood Heights Fire Company and the H. C. Pierce Hose Company will celebrate their century anniversaries in 2008. The police department, located for decades in the municipal building on Mountain Avenue, moved in June 2008 to a new $5 million state-of-the-art building located a short distance away from the municipal building. The Middlesex Borough Rescue Squad has been housed in the same building on Mountain Avenue since 1952.

Religious worship is offered in a number of churches located throughout the borough, including the Middlesex Bible Chapel, the Middlesex Kingdom Hall of Jehovah's Witnesses, the Middlesex Presbyterian Church, the Reorganized Church of Jesus Christ of Latter Day Saints, and Our Lady of Mount Virgin Roman Catholic Church.

The Middlesex Borough Elks was established in 1964 as lodge No. 2301. Its members are dedicated to promoting programs and support for disabled children and supporting families of children who face other serious health challenges. They are also dedicated to recognizing the youth of the borough for their scholastic, cocurricular, and athletic accomplishments.

Middlesex offers a wealth of programs for citizen involvement by all age groups, including the American Legion, the Veterans of Foreign Wars, the Red Hat Ladies group, a quilting group, church-related groups, afternoon and evening classes for adults, school-sponsored activities, plays and concerts, and a daily schedule of activities for senior citizens. Holiday parades, summer concerts by the New Jersey Symphony Orchestra, and a hometown picnic are also offered to the public. Citizens may serve as volunteers on numerous committees and boards for the overall betterment of the town and all it has to offer.

This second book on the history of Middlesex Borough is also done as a labor of love, and, to quote former mayor Joseph Zuccarelli, it is about "one of the best and biggest little towns in Central Jersey."

One

Remembering the Past

Pictured above are Walter and Laura Sisty with their best friend, Mitzi. They built the house they lived in on Vogel Place. Walter was a very talented individual who became a taxidermist. Presently the Senna family, which continues to appreciate the history this dwelling represents, occupies the house.

Former mayor Joseph Zuccarelli is pictured standing in front of the borough hall. In 1947, Middlesex Borough had purchased the Conover House, located at the northwest corner of Bound Brook Road and North Lincoln Boulevard. The house was remodeled to accommodate the municipal departments, including police, building, health, the council chamber, and the borough clerk. This house served the borough well until the construction of a brand-new borough hall on Mountain Avenue.

Middlesex Borough's entertainment pride, the Foothill Playhouse, provided summertime enjoyment in a rustic atmosphere. Emerging from behind a massive quilt curtain, players captivated audiences with new and old plays, dramas, comedies, and musicals. What a joy it was to be in *Camelot* in Middlesex. The property was sold in the 1980s, and while three lovely homes share the plot, the strains of *Camelot* can still be heard in the whispering of the trees.

A warm July day in Sparta was the perfect setting for a PTA outing. The ladies seem to enjoy being together in this beautiful place. The year was 1942 and World War II was challenging the citizens of this country. The PTA ladies, taking a few hours away from the war effort, had a history of caring for the children and serving free lunch during the hard times of the Depression so that every child could have at least one full meal a day.

Who can forget the classic lines of the old Pontiac parked in front of the Angelo Petty homestead at the corner of Madison Street and Voorhees Avenue? Joyce Ann Petty is dressed in her Sunday best for this picture. Notice the Plymouth parked behind the Pontiac. The only thing missing from the picture is the sight of Angelo sitting on the front porch.

This photograph was taken at the present borough hall. Pictured preparing the time capsule are three past mayors, all very dedicated volunteers who served the borough well, with pride and expertise. At left is Mayor Martin Matuszkiewicz, who served from 1970 to 1979. In the center is Mayor Joseph Zuccarelli, whose term was 1955 to 1956. On the right is Mayor Ronald Dobies, who served from 1980 to 2005. The three are preparing the time capsule for posterity.

John Haller (left) and Harry Peterson of the Middlesex Borough Sanitation Department are shown here disposing of some of the fish that were killed at Victor Crowell Park in the 1970s. Between 10,000 and 15,000 dead fish were reported in the lake from a pollution spill in a neighboring town, and members of the borough's sanitation department scooped up thousands of them and spread lime on the lake to lessen the odor and to help purify the water.

One of the earliest electrical contractors in town was Atomic Electric, a two-man operation conducted by Oreste "Rusty" DeSiato (left) and George Baker. DeSiato apprenticed as an electrician under Wilbur Smith, who operated Smith Electric in Bound Brook for many years. Atomic Electric was begun in the 1940s and continued well into the 1970s. Many of the older residents of town remember the prompt and courteous service they received from this company.

Ryan's Market, located on the corner of Route 28 and Shepherd Avenue, was one of the first convenience stores in Middlesex Borough. Walter Ryan (seen here) owned and operated this popular store during the 1950s. After his tenure as owner, the market was operated by his brother Frank Ryan. Later the property was sold to make room for an office building, which presently occupies the site.

The 1940s Efinger Bees softball team of Middlesex, above, had a record of 23-2. Pictured from left to right are (first row) mascots Ken Blair and Bob Schlick; (second row) Gene Schlick, Howie Walker, Herb Crowell, Lou Otto, and Charlie Senna; (third row) Dick Agans, George Carhart, John Powers, John Agans, Harry Gore, Ed Buckliew, and Bob Powers. The coaches were Carl Rabke and Bill Lawler. John Agans did all the pitching, and Senna caught every game.

The old barn on the westerly side of the property at the corner of Route 28 and Hazelwood Avenue was once the home of the pony Molly. The stall, hayrack, and hayloft were later remodeled, and the barn became the Colonial House Package Goods Store. A later transformation turned the package store into the Crouse Real Estate Agency. At present, the barn is a one-bedroom apartment.

Nicolina and Theodore Petty, the parents of Angelo Petty, take time out from celebrating Easter with their family to have a picture taken for posterity. The Petty family, which moved to Middlesex in 1914, is typical of the many Italian immigrants that came to Middlesex. These early immigrants assimilated with the Poles and the Irish to form the nucleus of the population, which helped to develop and nurture the town.

The 50th anniversary of the establishment of the borough of Middlesex was a cause for celebration. One of the many festivities was a parade commemorating the event. Fire engines, floats, bands, and marchers made the day memorable. Ernest Derby's milk delivery truck is pictured here on Lincoln Boulevard as the parade winds its way through the borough.

Shown in this picture is the Tagliaferro residence, the first house built on Ambrose Avenue. Also pictured is the family car, a 1953 Ford. The street was a dirt road in 1957, the year in which the house was completed. The Tagliaferros still reside at this residence.

Middlesex councilman Jasper Headley (left) and borough employee Harry Peterson are seen inspecting the Galion road grader, Middlesex's own "big machine." During the 1950s, Middlesex Borough built and maintained its roads. The picture location is the corner of Harris Avenue and Drake Avenue. Note the absence of houses.

In the early days of bare-knuckle prizefighting that involved contests lasting over 20 rounds at times, Bob Fitzsimmons stands out as one of the most famous fighters of all time. "Ruby Robert," as he was called, won three boxing championships, all by knockout, defeating Jack Dempsey in 1891 for the world middleweight crown and James J. "Gentleman Jim" Corbett in 1897 for the world heavyweight crown. He lost his heavyweight title to James J. Jeffries in 1899, but later, at age 40, he knocked out George Gardner in 20 rounds in 1903 to win the light heavyweight title. As a boy, Fitzsimmons worked as a blacksmith and, in 1906, purchased land in the Dewey Park section of Middlesex and plied his blacksmithing trade. He made souvenir horseshoes, which he sold to area residents. He won the world horseshoe-pitching championship. He had a pet lion called Senator, which he walked through the streets of Middlesex. After retiring from boxing, he toured the vaudeville circuit before becoming an evangelist. Fitzsimmons Street in Middlesex was named in his honor.

Nick Alimecco is at the microphone at a Veterans of Foreign Wars program in 2005, reliving and sharing his experiences as a soldier at Pearl Harbor on that "Day of Infamy," December 7, 1941. Alimecco and his wife raised their family on Parker Street where they have been residents since the early 1950s. Today this most active man of 89 years shares his military experiences not only with war veterans' groups but also with students at various grade levels.

In January 2007, a group of Middlesex women presented a historical quilt to the Middlesex Public Library. Each person had fashioned a quilt square representing some facet of borough history. Each square was designed and created in the unique style of its creator, using cross-stitch, appliqué, photographs, piecework, or paint. The topics for the designs were based on the Arcadia Publishing book of Middlesex history.

This attractive Tudor-style home is an example of some of the existing older homes in Middlesex Borough. In 1922, Charles Boast, a builder and craftsman, built several beautiful houses in Middlesex. He built this one, as lovely inside as out, for his family. Subsequent owners, the Stones and Korsgaards, called this Raritan Avenue brick house their home. It is currently the home of Beverly and Richard Weber.

Mayor Joseph Zuccarelli (left) and borough clerk Elmer Hoagland are observing work being done by Middlesex Road Department employees. The borough owned a grader and a steamroller and utilized them efficiently to provide the townspeople with excellent roads. Zuccarelli was mayor of the borough from 1955 to 1956. Elmer Hoagland was borough clerk for 29 years, retiring in 1972.

Shown in a 1967 photograph at Armond Patullo's Sinclair gas station at Bound Brook Road and Dayton Avenue are, from left to right, Ken Vaccaro, Jim Hower, and Tony Tarrantino. All three men learned their trade from Patullo. The buildings in the background are Massessa's Barber Shop and the Middlesex Bakery. The bakery property is now the site of Unity Bank.

Members of the Middlesex Borough Rescue Squad gathered as a group for this picture taken in the 1960s honoring Bob Canavan (front row, center) as their newly elected president. From left to right are (first row) Ray Rood, Louis Gearino, Bob Canavan, unidentified, and Platt Armstrong; (second row) Phil Ackerman, Andy Wnek, Harry Whalen, John De Gutis, John De Massari, Charles Semmer, and Andy Simpf.

Two

LEARNING FOR THE FUTURE

Winifred Bowlby stands proudly with her first-grade students for their class picture taken at Pierce School during the 1948–1949 school year. Bowlby was a first-grade teacher at Pierce School from 1947 to 1951. From 1963 through 1998, she taught kindergarten in a number of district schools, including Watchung, Central, the high school annex, and Hazelwood. After 39 years of dedicated service to the school district and students, she volunteered her skills teaching English as a second language to elementary students.

Peter Diskin began his long educational career at Middlesex High School in the fall of 1964 as a history teacher, head cross-country coach, and track coach. In 1967, he was appointed to the position of vice principal. He held the position of principal from 1978 to 1995. After retirement, Diskin served as a substitute teacher, resulting in his having three generations of students. When asked what his favorite Middlesex High School class was, he always responds, "I have the fondest of memories of all of them and I loved them all. I attempted to treat all students fairly and equally."

Here are the smiling faces of sixth graders at Pierce School during the 1959–1960 school year. Most of these students continued their education in Middlesex and became members of the Middlesex High School class of 1966. To the disappointment of many Middlesex residents, Pierce School closed its doors to learning in 1983.

Sue Baran retired in June 2005 after a lengthy teaching career in a number of district schools and various grade levels. Her career ended as a Von E. Mauger School teacher. She is pictured here as a Parker School teacher with her fifth-grade class during the 1983–1984 school year. Most of these students are members of the Middlesex High School class of 1991.

Members of the Middlesex High School class of 1967 are in the school gymnasium for the annual yearbook signing, a most popular event in that time period held days before graduation. *The Tempo* is the name of the yearbook, and, as one can observe here, classmates are exchanging written messages on their individual pictures as a lasting memento of the four years they spent together at Middlesex High School.

This group of Watchung School students during the 1954–1955 school year is totally involved in the social studies lesson on the contributions of various Native American tribes to American culture generally and, more specifically, to the Thanksgiving holiday. Note the headdresses of the students, the symbols of Native American tribes in the hands of the standing students, and the number of posters about the room, all joining together to enhance instruction.

Central School, now Von E. Mauger School, had its own band, which was under the direction of Dominick Pirone. A large number of the students participated in the band. All kinds of instruments from tubas to xylophones, drums, horns, and reed instruments were featured in the band. Pirone taught Middlesex students at all levels from the elementary schools through the high school.

Youngsters of Our Lady of Mount Virgin School are delighted with what they see during a special slide and sound three-dimensional presentation given by Studio 3-D. The show, a highlight of Catholic Schools Week in early February, included science, art, and history delivered through images that seemed to jump right off the screen. The children learned why it takes two eyes to see three-dimensional objects and much more about dimensions, imaging, and vision.

Teacher Shirley DeMiere sits with her smiling first-grade students at Hazelwood School during the 1972–1973 school year. Most of these students became members of the Middlesex High School class of 1984. Today DeMiere is known as Shirley Ekberg. She is presently the principal of Hazelwood School.

Smiling in front of their school, the 1949–1950 Watchung School faculty poses for the photographer. From left to right are (first row) Agnes C. Gall, Ruth R. Houston (principal), Harriet Hart, and Von E. Mauger (superintendent of Middlesex Schools); (second row) Nora K. Smith, Marion A. Ludgate, Helen S. Cookson, Marie E. Schubert, and Edna Titlar; (third row) Clementine A. M. Petit (secretary to superintendent), Edith C. Philhower, Beulah T. Wilson, Margaret K. Soroka, and Mrs. Teston (school nurse); (fourth row) Robert Vosbrinck, Richard I. Mewhinney, Herbert Kelshaw, and Norman J. Hawk.

The first cheerleading squad at Watchung School was instituted during the 1949–1950 school year. Pictured above are the proud members of the squad. From left to right are (first row) Diane Rustic and Sylvia Tolomeo (cocaptains); (second row) Constance Eberhart, Barbara Kerstetter, Helen Havens, and Elizabeth Scalzo. The girls are members of the eighth-grade class.

Shown here are the children in Connie Nicolay's second-grade class at Pierce School in 1959. The class size was typical for the late 1950s. There were two Pierce Schools in Middlesex: one was constructed in 1902 on the west side of Raritan Avenue, and the other was built on Walnut Street in 1921 at a cost of $118,000 and consisted of eight rooms. It replaced the original Pierce School.

Mayor Jasper Correnti (left) and school board president Stephen Bitow are displaying the Carl Y. Rabke Memorial Award. The award is presented annually to the outstanding boy and girl in the graduating class who demonstrated general excellence in their four years of high school studies in all subjects. The award was established in 1962, the first year that students graduated from Middlesex High School.

Holly Polakiewicz is shown here in 1998 ready for her first day of kindergarten at Our Lady of Mount Virgin School. It has served as Middlesex's only parochial school since its construction in the mid-1950s. Sunday masses were held in the school auditorium prior to the opening of the new Our Lady of Mount Virgin Roman Catholic Church on Harris Avenue in the early 1970s.

In 1953, the Watchung School band performed *HMS Pinafore* under the baton of Dominick Pirone. Music was a favorite class for many Middlesex students, probably because of the energetic and dynamic leadership of Pirone. The staging of the show was perfect, and the sound produced by the band was wonderful to hear.

This photograph of the 1956 Central School eighth-grade graduation shows the next-to-last class of Middlesex students who went to and graduated from Bound Brook High School. Construction began on Middlesex High School the year that members of this class were sophomores at Bound Brook High School in 1957. This class and the class of 1961, the last class of students from Middlesex to graduate from Bound Brook, ended an era when Middlesex students went to Bound Brook or earlier to Dunellen or Plainfield High Schools.

Clowning at Watchung School to promote student interest in reading are, from left to right, parents Terry Maxcy, Helen Stazo, and Bette Comune. The involvement of these mothers was part of a school program called I Like Me-Books and the larger-in-scope program Pioneers-Telecordia Chapter 99.

The members of the front office staff of Watchung School are all smiles in this early-1970s photograph. From left to right are (first row) school nurse Margaret Wolf and secretaries Jean Schroeder and Sara Mazze; (second row) vice principal Gene Vescia and principal Fred Vowinkel. Members of the staff spent the majority of their educational careers working in the Middlesex Schools system.

The Hazelwood elementary school, designed in 1964 by architect Norman W. Coates, opened in 1966. Rectangular in shape and located on one floor, it contained 17 classrooms, two of which were for kindergarten, and another was for "educable or trainable" students. This group of fourth graders poses for a class picture on May 7, 1971.

Our Lady of Mount Virgin School is completely paid for, and Fr. Joseph Fibner is all smiles as he puts a flame to the mortgage. Sharing the moment are Steve Dolgas (right) and William Heffernan (left). The year is 1986. The school continues to function today as an exceptionally good place for children to learn and become caring, contributing citizens.

Amybeth Waide is sitting fourth from the left in the first row during the June 1984 Von E. Mauger School graduation ceremony held in the high school gymnasium. Michelle Dorta is sitting at the extreme left, and Susan Crede is third from the left in the first row. The girls are showing their respect for their fellow eighth graders who have received their diplomas and are walking in front of them. Most students in this class are members of the Middlesex High School class of 1988.

The afternoon Pierce School kindergarten class during the 1956–1957 school year poses with its teacher for an annual group picture. Most of these students were members of the Middlesex High School class of 1969. Note the variety of pretty dresses worn by the girls and the number of bow ties worn by the boys. The first Pierce School opened in 1902, and the second Pierce School closed its doors in 1983.

Joe Diskin, the last student to receive his diploma during the class of 1983 commencement exercises, has his tassel moved from one side to the other by board of education president Robert Kizis. This action is done simultaneously by all of his fellow students as a symbol of their individual and group graduation from Middlesex High School on that June evening.

During 1957 and 1958, Middlesex High School was built. Middlesex High School students, then being educated in neighboring Bound Brook High School, were welcomed into their own secondary school. This picture was taken at the groundbreaking ceremony. Pictured are, from left to right, board member Steve Bitow, superintendent of schools Von E. Mauger and wife Ruth Mauger, Val Houska, board of education president Robert Kinstler, board member William Armstrong, and Steven Bates at the microphone. The first principal of the high school was Ruth Houston-Hollingsworth.

After the flood that followed Hurricane Floyd, Gov. Christine Todd Whitman visited stricken areas in the state, assessing the damages, both public and private. Whitman, in the light suit, is shown here at Our Lady of Mount Virgin School, talking with students, teachers, and parents.

The setting is the Middlesex High School cafeteria and town citizens and education officials have received certificates of merit as part of a board of education meeting. From left to right are Herb Wilson, Olin Thomas, Norman Hawk (assistant superintendent of schools), Jennie Sprinkle (editor of the *Middlesex Chronicle*), Ronald Dobies (board of education member and future mayor of Middlesex), Irene Thomas, and Thomas Schuyler (principal).

Superintendent of schools Dr. Virginia Brinson (left), school board president Ronald Dobies (second from right), and board member Josephine Tarulli welcome Seymour Weiss to the Middlesex School District as the new assistant superintendent of schools. The plain cinder-block walls and exposed pipes illustrate the economics practiced by the board of education in the mid-1970s.

Students of Our Lady of Mount Virgin School take a break from their studies for a photograph. The girls outnumber the boys, and it looks like everyone is having a good time. This is an eighth-grade honors algebra class in the spring of 1979.

Middlesex High School principal Peter Diskin stands with the outstanding athletes of the class of 1981 at the annual sports banquet in June of that year. From left to right are Jack Wilson, Donna Mooney, and James Petty. These athletes were three-sport participants and had tremendous athletic accomplishments during their careers.

Ruth Pohli is pictured here with her kindergarten class in 1971 at the Hazelwood elementary school. Pohli taught at Hazelwood for many years and is fondly remembered by her former students. There is hardly a Middlesex child of the 1970s and 1980s who did not march in costume with her kindergarten class at Halloween. Pohli, a favorite of the little ones and their parents, provided a sound educational background for Middlesex children for many years. Her enthusiasm, creativity, and love inspired children and parents alike.

The combined administrative, teaching, and support staffs of Parker School pose in the library for this 1988–1989 school year picture. Sitting at the extreme right is principal Phil Sidotti. Longtime school secretary Stella Andersen is standing second from the right. Sitting on the floor on the left is school nurse Margaret Wolf. All others pictured are teaching staff members.

On a rather chilly day in 1956, fourth-grade students in Parker School gathered with their teacher to have a class picture taken. Their teacher, a Mrs. Wolf, smiles proudly as she stands behind her class. Some of the boys are dressed ready for a Scout meeting later in the day. Parker School was one of the first schools in the borough, and its wide front doors are still welcoming young learners today.

It appears that Michael Canavan (left) and Paul Johnson are contemplating their next step up after elementary school. They were great friends throughout grade school at Our Lady of Mount Virgin School and in high school. Of like minds, both graduated from law school and are today both practicing attorneys. They are pleasantly surprised to meet in court or office on some matter. Both are married and live outside the Middlesex area.

Board members Bill Howes (center) and Steve Bitow are pictured here seated with students at a school board meeting at Central School in 1958. The students were participating in the Youth in Government program sponsored by the Middlesex Elks. In the program, students are assigned to a specific board member and learn the duties of the school board by attending a meeting and through discussion with their mentors.

Seated behind sturdy wooden desks on solid wooden chairs, Parker School second graders fold their arms and put on a happy smile. The year is 1954. The clothes, shoes, and hairstyles reflect the times. Serious learning was taking place here. Charts and books around the room show off some of the young people's work.

Charlie Weis, presently coach of the University of Notre Dame football, holds the interest of his audience at a Holy Name Society communion breakfast at Our Lady of Mount Virgin Roman Catholic Church in 1991. Listening are, from left to right, J. Dombroski, Rich Hoelzel, Jim Benson, Harry Werner, and Frank Bolonowski. Today Benson is chief of police in Middlesex.

Amybeth Waide is practicing her cheerleading technique in front of her home on Melrose Avenue. Like many girls in Middlesex, Waide started cheerleading in elementary school and continued through high school. The exercise is good, the uniforms are great, and the program has been very well run.

Regina Forgash was a fourth-grade teacher at Hazelwood School from the time it opened for instruction in 1966. Here she sits with her 1982–1983 fourth-grade class in the Hazelwood library. Forgash retired in 1995, always having a reputation of demanding the highest scholastic and behavior standards from her students. Most of these fourth graders are members of the Middlesex High School class of 1991.

Young Ray Romano stands obediently with his prayer book in hand on the day of his First Holy Communion in the spring of 1959. The picture was taken in front of Our Lady of Mount Virgin School, which was only four years old at the time. The Reverend Emanuel Gaucci was the church pastor and presided over the communion ceremony. Romano has the fondest of memories of growing up in town and was a graduate of the Middlesex High School class of 1970.

During the 1958–1959 school year, these Watchung School third-graders smile along with their teacher for the annual class picture. Most of these students were members of the Middlesex High School class of 1968.

The hills are alive, and *The Sound of Music* comes to life at Central School. The music was sweet, enthusiasm was high, and the production was a great success. Central School students worked many hours to perfect their interpretation of the classic. This photograph reflects the good time the students had in remembering and portraying the Von Trapp family singers.

Fourth-grade students at Our Lady of Mount Virgin School in Middlesex smile for the camera in 1975. Class picture day was an important day. Hairstyles and clothing reflect the colorful 1970s. At least three young men opted for the school uniform that day. Possibly they forgot that it was a necktie-free day.

In 1992, Our Lady of Mount Virgin Roman Catholic Church realized the need for a preschool program to begin the education of the young ones in the parish. The program, called Small Blessings, was initiated and continues to be very successful. Note the happy smiles on the faces of the children. In the early years of the school, sessions were two or three days per week, morning or afternoon, for two and a half hours each.

The first-grade students at Pierce School in 1977 are smiling for the camera and surround their teacher Shirley Hawk. Pictured are, from left to right, (first row) Jacob Bastardo, Barry Culver, Chad Fluks, Garry Frazes, and Michael Stazo; (second row) Vlasula Tsakiris, Angel Contursi, Lisa Kilian, Cynthia Gorman, Michelle Mergstt, teacher Shirley Hawk, Jessica Briggs, Tara Pella, Sheri Ulman, Susan Scanlon, and Barbara Paprzycki; (third row) Randy McConnell, Jeff Hesley, Dominic Mantuono, Jackie DeMassari, Kalliope Vallogeros, and Leann Bartlack.

Key people in the daily operation of a school are the secretaries. Pictured here is Barbara Cochran, secretary to high school principal Peter Diskin. Cochran's career at the high school spans the years 1963 to 1996. During that time period, she not only used her vast skills as every high school principal's secretary, but on a daily basis she also displayed total support and dedication to the staff and students.

High school principal Robert Vosbrinck (right) meets with his two assistant principals, Ronald Campbell (left) and Peter Diskin. The educational careers of this administrative trio spans close to 100 years of service in the Middlesex School District. Vosbrinck arrived at Central School in 1949 as a teacher and later served as principal of Central (Von E. Mauger) School and Middlesex High School, retiring in 1978. Campbell came to Central School in 1969 as a teacher and served later as assistant principal at Mauger and the high school. He was coordinator of secondary education, director of instruction for kindergarten through 12th grade, and superintendent of schools from 1981 to 1994.

Members of the Middlesex High School class of 1981 celebrate the completion of the graduation ceremony in June of that year with mutual applause for each other and the hoisting of balloons and their caps. The ceremony was held on the football field. Seen in this picture are Michael Venuto, a current borough councilman, and Scott Young, now a ranking member of the police department.

Whether it was a typical blustery day with abundant snow for sledding or a calm, sunny day with green grass, these Pierce School boys seem to be very happy in their own snowy holiday atmosphere.

Most of these third graders from Pierce School grew up to be part of the Middlesex High School class of 1969. With their hands neatly folded, dressed for picture day, and eyes on the photographer, the children seem to be enjoying the process. The classroom is well decorated, and the environment appears to be one of serious study.

Head Middlesex High School football coach Paul Murphy presents a plaque of recognition to Emil Bontempo, a member of the class of 1983, and the state Group I champion football team. Middlesex football teams, under the leadership of Murphy, won three state football championships during a five-year period in the early and mid-1980s. The 1974 team was the state Group II champion that year. Murphy had a lengthy and successful teaching and coaching career at Middlesex High School.

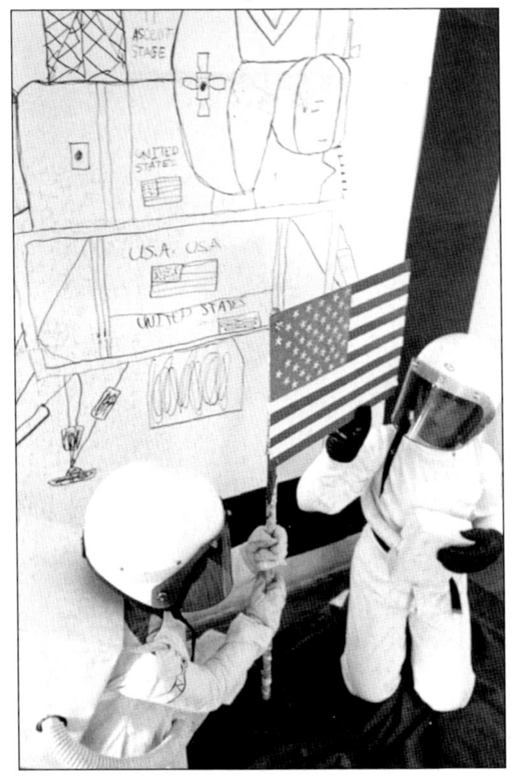

Harry Heinhold and John Markle, 10-year-old students at Pierce School in 1976, pay tribute to America's space program as part of a school project, the Flag of Our Country. The boys in their astronaut suits and the artwork added to the meaning of their project. It was also the year of the bicentennial celebration in America.

Three

PLAYING TOGETHER

Billy Gazi is getting ready to hit that homer for his team. Gazi is the son of former Middlesex Borough municipal attorney Bill Gazi and Mary Ann Gazi. He was a member of the 1982 Middlesex Little League Cubs team. Each team member had his own individual baseball card with his or her picture on it. This made them feel like real major leaguers. The team featured Barbara Levonitis at shortstop, the first girl to play in the Middlesex Little League.

Camelot came alive on the stage of the Foothill Playhouse on a balmy summer evening. This and an eclectic mix of productions brought pleasure to Middlesex Borough theatergoers for many seasons.

Earl DeSiato ranks as one of the best in the nation for hydroplaning, taking fourth place at the Stock/Modified/National Hydroplane Championships in July 2006. A hydroplane boat, powered by an engine and a propeller, is typically built to trap air under the hull. This trapping of air causes the boat to travel above the water's surface at top speed by hydroplaning.

Paul Butera, Special Olympics medalist, is pictured proudly wearing some of his many medals. He won two gold medals at the 1987 international games, five silver medals at the 1991 world summer games, a silver medal at the United States Special Olympic Games in 1993, and three gold medals at the first national games in 2006. Butera has been recognized as an Outstanding Citizen of Middlesex Borough and was named Outstanding Athlete of New Jersey by former governor Christine Todd Whitman.

On July 15, 2004, the Blooming Violets of the Red Hat Ladies Society met for tea at the home of queen mum Eleanore Matthiessen. Posing for a photograph are, from left to right, (first row) Ann Butera, Mary Elizabeth Conners, Theresa Boyd, Rita Nulty, Eleanore Matthiessen, and Barbara Morecraft; (second row) Joan Golias, Grace Pepe, Sharon Connors, Peggy Griffin, Cathy Lucchesi, Lillian Monterosa, Bea Dessino, Sarah Mazze, Maryann Zakashefski, Lottie Murray, Mel Renick, and Bette Comune; (third row) Mary Diskin, Lorraine Mazur, Estelle Gaullas, and Alice McIntrye.

The Pirates of the Middlesex Little League are pictured here in 1969 with their head coach John Martino (left) and assistant coach John Hreha. New York Mets second baseman Ken Boswell was guest speaker at the Little League's banquet that November, not long after the Mets won the World Series.

James Fiorentino, a unique, talented, and skilled artist, is a 1996 graduate of Middlesex High School, who, at age 15, was the youngest person to have a painting displayed in the National Baseball Hall of Fame. The likeness was of Reggie Jackson. He has been recommended to paint sport legends Ted Williams, Mickey Mantle, Cal Ripkin Jr., Muhammad Ali, Brett Favre, and countless others. He was also an outstanding shortstop on his high school and Drew University teams.

In the playground behind Our Lady of Mount Virgin School, a special magic happened in June 2002. The annual carnival, a delight for children and adults, was a major fund-raiser for the school. Food, games of chance, carnival rides, and music provided carnival-goers with hours of fun and a chance to socialize with friends.

Senior citizens group members from Our Lady of Mount Virgin Roman Catholic Church celebrate on a trip to the Dixie Stampede in Myrtle Beach, South Carolina. The local Catholic Church has sponsored its own senior citizens club for many years and the members go on trips and have monthly meetings. They enjoy each other's companionship. These seniors are always on the go and have great times together.

The 1955–1956 Central School basketball team is pictured above. From left to right are (first row) Tom Ireland, John Sweeney, Alex Morecraft, Art Poremba, and Art Morecraft; (second row) coach Norman Hawk, Mike Mauro, Charlie Matthews, Jim Pervy, Bob Boccadutre, Doug Condon, coach Frank Vicendese, and Claude Abondonte. Tom Stefanik, a member of the team, is not pictured.

The 1990 Middlesex High School baseball team won the 1990 Group I state championship in dramatic fashion, defeating New Providence High School 1-0, scoring on a squeeze play bunt in the last inning. From left to right are (first row) Alan Cheney, Kurt Lapari, Roger Nepton, John DeDominicis, and Jason Laub; (second row) Craig Cerrat, coach Bob Poeltler, Dave Hopeck, and Brian Parenti; (third row) Barry Moraller, Chris Lemley, Joe Schaline, Jeff Roy, assistant coach John DeCola, Jason Pena, and Pat Fay.

Paige Price, a member of the Middlesex High School class of 1982, has been cast in various roles as a Hollywood actress, Broadway star and performer, feature dancer, show producer, concert producer, and singer. On Broadway, Price has performed in *Beauty and the Beast* and *Smokey Joe's Café*. She had a starring role in *Saturday Night Fever*. Her film and television appearances include *All the Right Moves*, *The New Kids*, and *Newhart*. Mayor Michael Bloomberg proclaimed July 6, 2002, as Paige Price Day in New York City.

In 1949, the Watchung grammar school had its first basketball team. Robert Vosbrinck came to Middlesex as a physical education teacher that year. Since he had played basketball at Ithaca College, he volunteered to coach the team. The official (unidentified) looks like he is ready to call a foul on the Milford player (unidentified) as, from left to right, Dick Amy, Robert Ferris, and Rudy Wavershak close in on the ball carrier.

John Rafferty Jr. and his cousin Frances Rafferty are enjoying a ride on their hobbyhorse in 1954. John was the son of Mayor John Rafferty. Frances (now Esposito) was the daughter of Mayor Walter L. Rafferty. Their aunt was Helen Quelet, who for many years was the welfare director of the borough of Middlesex.

Dieter Schmidt has been racing big-block modified stock cars in competitions ranging from Florida to New England since 1992. He is one of the most successful owners in the racing circuit. In his spare time, he owns and operates Lincoln Auto Body Shop on Harris Avenue. His assistant, Leila Hancock, manages the body shop when Schmidt travels the racetrack circuit.

Jeff Maree, son of Charles and Barbara Maree, played football for Middlesex High School in 1983 and later starred as a safety on the University of Southern California football team where he played with Rodney Peete, the quarterback from 1984 to 1987. Maree now operates his own landscaping business and provides services to many Middlesex families.

Michelle Creighton (left) and teammate Lindsay Hopper are taking a time-out for a cool drink on a hot summer day. Both are members of the 1994 Middlesex Borough Small Fry baseball league. The girls played on the team for seven- and eight-year-olds. Less competitive than some teams, Small Fry teams gave children maximum pleasure with minimum stress. The biggest problem was, as Creighton said, "It was too hot in the outfield."

Steve Fellin gave 43 years of dedicated service to the Middlesex Little League. He was the epitome of the Little League qualities of character, courage, and loyalty not only in his role as longtime manager of the Reds but also in the various positions he held through the years. This man set the highest example for his fellow managers, coaches, and their players. The playing field is named in his honor and his memory. The 2004 season was dedicated to him.

In 2004, the Middlesex Lady Blue Jays softball team won the Group I state championship. In the final game, the Lady Blue Jays defeated Cedar Grove by a score of 10-0 to take the title. They are shown here in a team photograph, smiling and proud of their accomplishment.

Every spring, the Middlesex Little League comes to life. Each year, volunteers work diligently for many hours to give the youth of Middlesex the opportunity to play organized baseball. In 2000, Steve Fellin, the manager of the Reds, coached Jeff Creighton (left) and Pete Donhauser along with the other team members. The chance to participate in sports is a treat for the youngsters.

Members of the Middlesex Borough Elks Lodge No. 2301 enjoy the sun and each other's company at the Elks state convention held in Wildwood in June 1964. This was their first state convention as a Middlesex lodge because it was also instituted the same year. The Middlesex lodge is active today in initiating and supporting programs for disabled children and recognizing students at all grade levels for their scholastic and cocurricular activities.

Middlesex friends celebrate the wedding of Stephen Johnson and Ann Grasso. From left to right are (first row) Joan Mason, George Mason, Dr. Mohamed Sadaty, and Alba Sadaty; (second row) Humberto Monteferranti, Luisa Monteferranti, Stephen Johnson, Ann Grasso Johnson, and Elsa Renda. Mike Renda is behind the camera taking the picture. The Masons now live in California, the Sadatys are in Florida, and the Johnsons live in Georgia.

Kerwin's Tavern has been a local landmark in Middlesex for over 70 years. The original owner, Mike Kerwin, retired. His son Tim, who carries on the Irish tradition, now operates the business. Corned beef and cabbage on St. Patrick's Day is standard fare if one can get into the tavern on that day. Good food, good cheer, good company, and good music are featured at Kerwin's.

The Little League clubhouse is part of the Steve Fellin playing field complex located at Pierrepont and Wellington Avenues. In 2008, the clubhouse was named in honor of Bob Green for his years of dedication as the Pirates manager, a coach in his earlier years in the program, and for various positions he held on the Little League board. Green and others like him worked tirelessly to teach and improve the baseball knowledge and skills of their players.

In 1976, the Middlesex Fire Department sponsored a mustache contest as part of the Middlesex Borough 50th anniversary celebration. Several of the firemen grew mustaches, and the eventual winner of the event was George Hatfield. He is pictured in the center of the first row, with Chief George Schaub looking over his right shoulder (center, rear).

Enjoying a festive dinner together, members of the Middlesex Junior Women's Club appear to be eagerly planning their next endeavor. Club members, women between the ages of 18 and 35, spent their energies helping others through various projects, such as awarding scholarships to students and providing holiday meals for the needy. Members of the Middlesex Women's Club acted as advisors. Well remembered in this capacity are Lib Howes and Emily Osterman.

Mountainview Park in Middlesex comes alive on the Fourth of July. Families picnic together and with friends. Children play organized games. There are booths, music, and flags. On this occasion, the Middlesex Borough Heritage Committee mans a booth and offers the first Middlesex picture history book from Arcadia Publishing to a very receptive group.

From left to right, Chuckie, Jeff, Natalie, and Rodney Maree are pictured here enjoying a night out on the town. The Marees grew up in Middlesex, attending Middlesex schools. The boys helped their father with his landscaping business once they could walk. Now each has his own business, and all are doing well. Charles and Barbara Maree ensured their children's future by educating them well, and they are a credit to their parents.

Sailor hats apparently were in vogue in 1970 when this picture was taken. The car on the left looks like a racing car and the other looks like a box. Despite the advantage of aerodynamics, which should go to the racer, it looks like a dead heat. The secret must be in the leg muscles pushing those pedals.

A three-year-old's birthday wonder and excitement can hardly be contained by little Jim Liming. The year is 1978. Liming's big sister Karen is eager and ready to help him open all those gifts and maybe help him play with them also. The colorful gift wrappings almost match her shirt.

Samantha Gaffney appears a little apprehensive as Denise (Martin) Gaffney and Santa tell her tales of sugar plums and Christmas elves. Santa's other name is Bill Medler, a Middlesex resident and local businessman. Hopefully Samantha's Christmas morning was a delight. Most likely her grandparents Robert and Patricia Martin made sure that Santa did a good job.

From left to right, Jim Liming, Mary Jo Ferraro, and Laura Liming are having a grand time at their campsite in 1981. Many Middlesex families enjoy the outdoor world in the summers, hiking, camping, and picnicking in the many beautiful parks in New Jersey. Middlesex itself has many recreational areas and places for picnics, ball games, horseshoe pitching, swimming, tennis, and, of course, kiddie playgrounds.

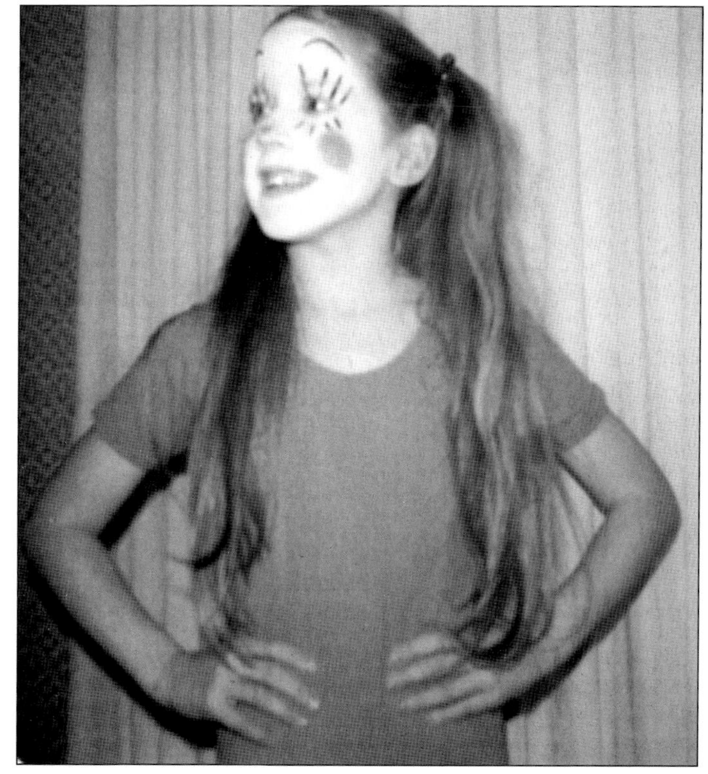

Ten-year-old Jenny Johnson waits with a painted clown face for the signal to go onstage in the 1977 New Jersey Ballet production of *The Nutcracker*. Johnson began her ballet training with Trudie Suabedissen of Middlesex and continued with the New Jersey Ballet School. Finally her dancing feet propelled her to a career as a special education teacher, happy wife to Bob, and mom to Jackie and Sean.

Bob and Sarah Martin are joined by a rather large friend. They are enjoying a family trip to Disney World. Bob is the son of Patricia and Robert Martin, longtime Middlesex residents. Robert Martin was a dockworker, and Patricia worked as a preschool aide and later as a legal secretary for Edward Johnson Jr.

George Vuolde, pictured here, lived on Ashland Road and enjoyed the company of neighboring children from the DeAngelis, Harac, and Ferris families. In the winter, George and his sisters Gina and Vicky built snowmen and snow forts and went sledding and skating in Victor Crowell Park with their friends. In the summer, Pierce School playground was near, and the Ambrose Brook was another attraction.

As the bride opens gifts off camera, the guests at this bridal shower are watching with varying degrees of interest and enthusiasm. From left to right are Julie Gregory, Karen Mason, Alba Sadaty, Joan Mason, Karen Johnson, Mildred Johnson, and Anne Bambo. The party was a huge success.

Fannie Heard McCollum and Aaron McCollum are enjoying a light repast and do not seem to mind the interruption as they pose for this picture. This was obviously a happy occasion, as evidenced by their smiling faces.

The 1982 Middlesex Little League Cubs were coached by, from left to right, Eugene Sillib, Raymond Levonitis, and Len McDougal. These Little League ballplayers are now young adults.

Softball provided an outlet for these girls in 1984. They enjoyed the camaraderie that playing together afforded them, and they displayed the school spirit that infused their extracurricular activities.

This picture seems to be planned, does it not? The height difference is fairly uniform, and the smiles are of the same intensity. It appears that a special occasion is the reason for this picture to be taken in 1986. It would be interesting to see the same group posing in the same fashion today.

The Mulrooney children gather together for a family portrait celebrating their parents' 40th wedding anniversary in December 1998. Notice the different collars, with Margaret (left) and Cathy wearing traditional white shirts, Mary in a mock turtle neck, Helen in a jewel neck, Tom (left) and Robert with no collars, and Jim with a full turtle neck.

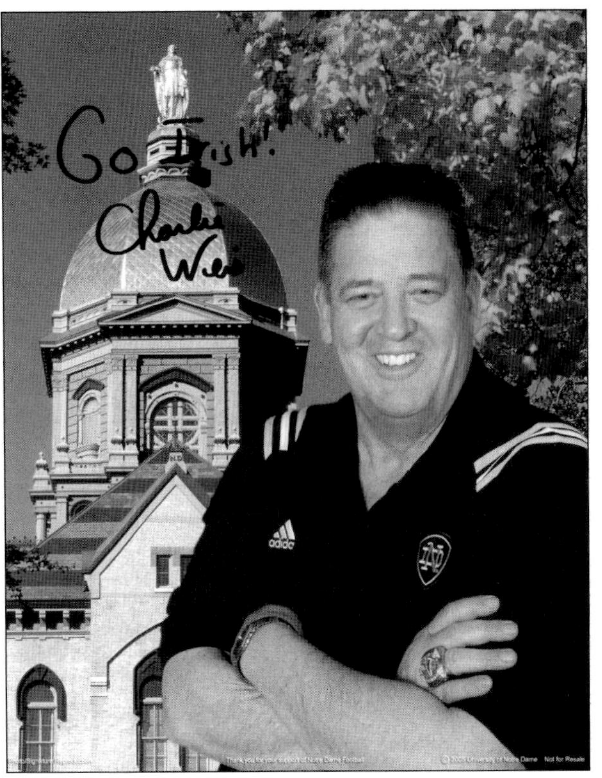

Charlie Weis, pictured, was a 1974 graduate of Middlesex High School. He graduated from the University of Notre Dame in 1978. He is presently head football coach of the Notre Dame Fighting Irish. Weis is the proud owner of four Super Bowl rings as a result of his 15 years as assistant coach for the New York Giants and the New England Patriots.

This 1952 photograph shows all the players on the four original Middlesex Little League teams and their coaches gathered together at the first Little League field on Harris Avenue. The teams were the Giants, the Dodgers, the Braves, and the Phillies. The teams still compete today, but the present team members may be grandsons, and the original sponsors are now only fond memories.

Little League players need coaches to teach them the fundamentals of the game and, even more important, the values of good sportsmanship. Teams cannot exist without coaches, and since there are so many pictures in this book of various teams, it is only fitting and proper that recognition is also given to those people who unselfishly give of their time and talents to help transform these kids into responsible and caring adults.

In 1986, this group advanced to the finals of the state tournament for 12-year-olds before tasting the agony of defeat. From left to right are (first row) Jayson Laub, Keith Glenfield, Tom Dyrness, Scott Cheney, Jonathan Adamski, Frank Travisano, Brian Feath, Troy Armenti, and Brian Parenti; (second row) manager Bob Green, Tom Olsen, John Galiardi, David Hopeck, Chris Balent, Tom King, and coach Dick Lauler.

In the 1970s, the Middlesex Jaycees challenged the mayor and council to baseball games. The games were enjoyed by players and spectators. The photographer took this picture through the fence to get a good view of the batter. It looks like he is ready to slam a home run. This game was one of many community activities that brought the people of Middlesex together and helped to increase the small-town feeling among residents.

Members of the Middlesex Borough Elks Lodge No. 2301 march next to their Crippled Children Bank float during the 75th anniversary of Middlesex parade in 1988. Middlesex was incorporated as a town in 1913. On the day of the parade, large crowds lined both sides of Bound Brook Road to get a good view. All residents enjoyed the many activities of the day. The Elks continue to be active and enthusiastic in their efforts to make the world a better place.

Four

GROWING AND CHANGING

The stately Colonial House is believed to be the oldest building in the borough of Middlesex. From 1930 to 1970, the building housed the Colonial House Restaurant, owned and operated by Thomas Mullin. In the 1950s, Bill Crouse, Joe Yarnell, and other local businessmen played music at the restaurant. The building now is the home of a child care center, but in its heyday, it was one of the better-known restaurants in the area.

The old Seifert barn, which was located off Warrenville Road, changed with the times. The barn was part of the Seifert farm, which featured a stately old house facing Warrenville Road and a large field on which various crops were planted. Today a small housing development has replaced the farm, and the old barn is just a fleeting memory.

This looks like a lovely split-level residence on the corner of Greenbrook Road and Route 28. In reality, this is the law office of Edward Johnson Sr. and his sons Edward Jr. and Robert. The building was constructed in the early 1970s and still graces the corner. The Johnson sons carry on their father's tradition. Two of Edward Jr.'s sons, Stephen and Paul, and Robert's daughter Wendy chose careers in law.

Pictured above is the original retail establishment owned by the Biondi family. This photograph was taken in the spring of 1966. The garden center and flower shop have been refurbished and modernized to accommodate the increase in business. They have developed a reputation for quality and service second to none. Phil and Mae Biondi carry on the family tradition, and their son Glen and daughter Alyson Rau are also following in their footsteps.

Guy and Carol Hoyt provide Christmas joy to hundreds of sightseers each year with their fantastic window and house decorations. Animated dolls and animals provide companionship for Santa in the snowy winter wonderland. It transforms the house into a miniature FAO Schwartz store during the Christmas season. Visitors are encouraged to get a close-up view of the decorations. They come from miles away to see the displays.

Middlesex Borough eagerly welcomed a shopping center on Union Avenue in the 1960s. An A&P grocery store and W. T. Grants department store shared the space with various smaller stores. When Grants closed, Shepards became Middlesex's store of choice, supplying most of residents' needs, real and imagined. The parking lot was always full. Later Shepards passed the torch to Drug Fair, which holds its place today, offering prescription drugs and household needs.

This trio provides friendly service to patrons of the Exxon gasoline station at the corner of Route 28 and Greenbrook Road. Darren Moreno helps his father with repairs. Callistus "John" Moreno is the master mechanic, and Billy Singh pumps the petrol. The Morenos commute each day from Newark. Billy moved to Middlesex from India. Cheerful service is dispensed liberally at the station, and the repair work is top-notch.

Members of the Middlesex Borough Rescue Squad are pictured in front of the squad building on Mountain Avenue in this 1960s picture. From left to right are (first row) Jessie Apgar, Andy Wnek, unidentified, unidentified, Joe Eagan, Ray Rood, Harry Whalen, Leonard Winters, and Charles Semmer; (second row) Paul Kulpak, Charles Stazo, Al Kelly, Ray Martin, Lou Gearino, Frank Conrad, Don Ellery, unidentified, Michael Trerotola, Frank Guibleo, Platt Armstrong, John Tomasetti, Gavin Flanagan, and Phil Ackerman.

Pictured here are the current members of the Middlesex Borough Rescue Squad. The squad is a nonprofit corporation that was established to provide first aid to sick, injured, and disabled persons and to provide transportation to and from accident scenes and from homes to area hospitals. All members are nonpaid volunteers. In 2008, there were 29 active members, 16 of whom were qualified emergency medical technicians. In 2007, the squad answered over 900 calls for assistance.

Jake, Gina, and Tony Qiku have been serving fine food at Carpaccio Ristorante since 1976, when they and their brother John purchased Bambo's Oxbow Steakhouse. In 1987, the name was changed to Carpaccio Ristorante. The three brothers and Jake's wife, Gina, immigrated to the United States from Albania in 1968. They worked at area restaurants and saved their money so they could start their own business. Their restaurant is famous for fine food and service. In the picture are, from left to right, Tony, Gina, and Jake.

Keith Kermizian started in the carpet business with his father, Vahe Kermizian, in Bound Brook in 1954 but expanded the business to include tile and wood flooring when the operation was relocated to Bound Brook Road in Middlesex in 1957. Keith's mother, Edna "Carol" Kermizian, manages the store during the day while Keith installs carpets, tile, and wood flooring. Kermizian's is the longest continuous sponsor of Little League teams in the borough.

Steve, George, Kevin, and Marie Mavrianos moved from Greece to New Jersey in 1968. They purchased the Mountainview Diner in September 1988 and have operated the restaurant since that time. They celebrated their 20th anniversary in 2008. They have survived three floods that destroyed the restaurant, but they rebuilt each time. Kevin moved back to Greece in 1996. The Mavrianos family is known and loved by all who patronize this friendly establishment. Pictured are, from left to right, Steve, Marie, and George.

The staff of Middlesex Texas Weiner Restaurant is anxious to please the customers, and a friendly smile and fast service is their trademark. The family restaurant is located in the center of town across from the shopping center. Tony Kamarinopolis (the man with the tie) started the restaurant when the Hardee's restaurant closed at this location. The business is now being operated by his son Paul and Paul's friend Tony Chatzapoulos.

The very popular Ellery's Restaurant and Pub, located on the corner of Lincoln Boulevard and Mountain Avenue on the site of the former Hotel Lincoln, opened its doors to the public for the first time in March 1997. The proud owners are John Ellery, a member of the Middlesex High School class of 1979, and his wife. They advertise their business as one of the finest and friendliest family dining spots in Middlesex County. Orders to go, catering, a busy pub, lunch, and dinner are all parts of the restaurant's offerings.

The enticing smell of french fries lured hungry Middlesex residents into the favorite fast-food place Hardee's in the 1970s. Previously the corner was the site of the Manor House, an early Middlesex restaurant. Eventually Hardee's left Middlesex and the present-day Middlesex Texas Weiner restaurant still provides great french fry smells and other wonderful odors to bring customers flocking.

Middlesex has a tradition of people staying. Many borough residents decided to expand upward rather than move out of town when they needed additional room for their growing families. Typical of this expansion is the Waide house on Melrose Avenue, which expanded from a Cape Cod bungalow to a two-story Colonial. Joe and Agnes Waide contracted with Jack DeAngelis, a local builder and longtime borough resident, to do the house addition during the winter, which was not the most propitious time for such a project. The weather was cold at the time, and a snowstorm was imminent. Getting the addition completed in a hurry was essential. DeAngelis completed installing the roof for the new second floor in just one day, thereby assuaging the fears and concerns of the owners and assuring himself of their everlasting gratitude.

Delta Cleaners, located at the corner of Route 28 and Harris Avenue, has been in business since 2000. This location featured gasoline stations in the past. The store abuts the Quick Check Shopping Center. The current owners immigrated to the United States from Korea. There are many retail establishments in Middlesex Borough that are owned and operated by recent immigrants who have embraced the community and adapted well to their new environment. America remains the land of opportunity.

Eric Troia, his wife, Ingrid, and son Mario are pictured in front of their new restaurant on Union Avenue, known as Pizza Center Restaurant. The Troia family formerly operated the Pizza Center Restaurant at the Middlesex Shopping Center for many years before moving to its new location. The restaurant features a full-service menu and casual-dining facilities. At the shopping center location, pizza was the main feature, but at the expanded venue, full-course dinners are the specialty.

Five

Celebrating Family

From left to right, T. J., Laura, Catherine, and Jimmy Kerwin are the children of Tim and Betsy Kerwin, and this picture was used on their 2007 Christmas card. The Kerwin family has roots in Middlesex and in this area. Catherine has started acting in her spare time at the Franklin Township Villagers Theater, and the boys are kept busy in local sports activities, while little Laura enjoys the attention of her big brothers and sister.

Pictured in the gardens are Peter and Edythe (Scott) Staffelli of Hazelwood Avenue. Edythe was born in Jersey City, and Peter was born in Plainfield. Peter's father, Louis Staffelli, was mayor of Middlesex during the 1950s. In 1955, Edythe moved to Seaside Heights. On the boardwalk, her summer friends introduced her to Nina Staffelli, who told Edythe about her brother Peter. They met, but nothing clicked. However, the next meeting in 1956 did click.

The Peter and Fran Ciliberto family celebrate at the shore. The Cilibertos moved to Middlesex in 1964. Their 5 children and 17 grandchildren are pictured here enjoying a family vacation. Four of the families still live in Middlesex. This is fairly typical, as many of the children who grew up in town liked it so much that they either stayed here or moved back after living somewhere else.

A typical family celebration is always a good time. This one in June 1983 is honoring Luigi Renda, who moved with his family from Italy to Argentina and then to Middlesex. Renda is typical of the many immigrants who moved to Middlesex, got jobs, made a good living, raised and educated a family, and helped make Middlesex Borough a great place to live.

Sylvester C. Pitt, son of Middlesex resident Leshanda "Mae" Pitt, is beaming with pride, posing for a picture with his daughter Sonja and his grandchildren Alia and Miya. What a lucky man to be the recipient of so much obvious love. Mae is known and loved in the borough for her many good works. Show her a lonely person and she will cook a meal for them and bring them a bit of happiness. Her family reflects her goodness.

Clyde and Priscilla Fisk are enjoying a vacation attending a convention, but the location is unknown. Clyde was the Middlesex Borough engineer for many years and enjoyed fixing clocks as his avocation. He established the firm Fisk Associates, which is continued today by his sons Paul and Steve Fisk, who carry on the tradition of excellence established by their father.

Standing proudly with his 12 children is Walter Rutkowski, a longtime resident of Middlesex Borough. From left to right are (first row) Denise, Walter, Maryann, and Gary; (second row) John, Mark, Kenneth, Robert, and Joseph; (third row) James, William, Richard, and Thomas.

The Mastrull family first moved to Middlesex in 1963. From left to right are (first row) Jill, Buddy, Barbara, and Jane; (second row) Jeff and Joey. Barbara and Buddy were high school sweethearts, king and queen of their prom, and graduates of the Bound Brook High School class of 1953. Barbara worked as a secretary at Middlesex High School, and Jill is presently an English teacher there.

Pictured here in Atlantic City is Mary Oliver with son David's family, who has resided at the corner of Ashland Road and B Street for more than 35 years. David's wife Marion taught at Von E. Mauger School for 25 years. David taught and coached at Middlesex High School in the 1960s and 1970s. He served two terms as a councilman and three as a board of education member. Their sons David and Matt graduated from Middlesex High School. David is a successful entrepreneur, and Matt is an attorney.

Carmella and Nicholas Alimecco pose with their daughters Dolores and Rosary in the 1950s. The Alimeccos are longtime residents of Parker Street. Carmella worked for years in the high school cafeteria. Nicholas served in the army and was at Pearl Harbor on December 7, 1941. Rosary is a teacher at Our Lady of Mount Virgin School. Dolores resides out of state.

This 1950 photograph shows Elida Morecraft with her nine children, William, Maude Pederson, Herbert, Kenneth, Lillian, Elwood, Eliza Peltz, Gladys, and Virginia Santoman at the family's traditional Thanksgiving dinner at her home on Union Avenue. Also pictured are the wives, husbands, grandchildren, and invited guests of the Morecrafts.

Pictured are Arch J. and Elsa Ferris. Elsa was the daughter of William and Nance Morrison and married Arch Ferris in 1933. Arch managed the William L. Finck Greenhouses on Union Avenue until April 1, 1951. At that time, he opened Ferris Brothers Wholesale Florist, which still operates at 565 Union Avenue in Middlesex. This picture was taken at their 50th wedding anniversary.

Walter and Helen Paul were the first occupants of a Cape Cod home at 432 First Street. The $11,500 home was purchased under the GI Bill in 1955 with a $500 down payment. Helen is shown here in front of the property with her children, four-year-old Carolyn, three-year-old Barbara, two-year-old Walter Jr., and one-year-old Arthur.

Catherine and Thomas Mulrooney are pictured at their wedding in Brooklyn, New York. After their marriage, they moved to Middlesex Borough, where they raised their children, who all attended school in Middlesex. Tom worked as a banker in New York City. Both Catherine and Thomas were very active in activities at Our Lady of Mount Virgin church and school in Middlesex.

Ed and Mary Lou Johnson are all smiles at their daughter Jenny's wedding to Bob Emrich. Ed, a lifelong Middlesex resident, lawyer, borough attorney, and former school board and library board member, met Minnesotan mathematics teacher Mary Lou in Bound Brook. They married and raised four children, Greg, Steve, Paul, and Jenny. Mary Lou taught mathematics for 27 years at Immaculata High School. Together they formed the Middlesex Borough Heritage Committee to create two picture histories.

Ronald and Blanche Dobies and their family have lived in Middlesex since the early 1960s. Their daughters Mary and Patricia both went to Parker School and graduated from Middlesex High School. Pictured here during a vacation in Florida are, from left to right, (first row) Trevor Tomczak, Mallory Drake, Steven Drake, and Tyler Tomczak; (second row) Patricia Tomczak, Mark Tomczak, Paul Drake, Mary Drake, Ronald Dobies, and Blanche Dobies.

Joseph J. and Agnes Waide moved to Middlesex in 1962. Joseph served as a member of the Middlesex Borough Planning Board for many years. A family photograph at Christmas catches the joy of the season. From left to right are (first row) Chuck Cowell, mom Agnes, Amybeth, Jim Gorman, James Gorman, Joseph D. Waide, and dad Joseph J. Waide; (second row) Brian, Justin, Joseph S. Waide, Natalie, Kevin, Michele, Jeremy Waide, and Wade Cowell.

Charles and Barbara Maree are longtime residents of Middlesex Borough. They raised their daughter and three sons, all of whom completed higher education at the urging of their parents. Charles had a full-time job but also spent 40 hours each week operating his landscaping business. Daughter Natalie is pictured with her parents.

Walter Figel and his wife, Evelyn, raised their family on Melrose Avenue. The six Figel children are Joyce, Walter, Kenny, Audrey, Rosemary, and Anthony. Walter and Evelyn were also equally proud of their grandchildren. Walter had a lengthy career as a physical education and health teacher at Pierce, Watchung, and Central (Von E. Mauger) Schools. Walter was an outstanding athlete at Bound Brook High School, always known as "Brookie No. 21."

Peter and Mary Diskin are 42-year residents of Middlesex. Peter's career as an educator was entirely at Middlesex High School in the roles of teacher, coach, and administrator. In retirement, he is a substitute teacher in all of the borough schools. Mary is known for her talented and creative crafts and quilting skills. The Diskin children are all graduates of Middlesex High School. Pictured from left to right are (first row) Brian and Joseph; (second row) Peter Jr., Mary, Peter Sr., and Patricia.

The Ferris family has lived in Middlesex since 1965, first residing on Ashland Road and then on Hazelwood Avenue. Pictured here are Robert and Catherine Ferris with sons Robert (center) and Jay and daughters Kathleen (left) and Karen. All the children were active in Pierce, Hazelwood, and Von E. Mauger Schools and graduated from Middlesex High School.

This picture of the Ritchie children was a 40th wedding anniversary present to their parents, Jack and Claire Ritchie. The Ritchies were longtime residents of Walnut Street. Jack was a World War II veteran and postal worker in Bound Brook for many years. Claire is a housewife and still-loving matriarch. From left to right are (first row) Mark, Mary (sitting), and Thomas; (second row) Jim, John, and Patricia.

Rita and Phil Lopa, pictured here celebrating their 25th wedding anniversary, were high school sweethearts at Bound Brook High School. After their marriage, they lived in Bound Brook before moving to a house in Middlesex. Phil began his career as an electrician, and later, as a contractor, he helped to make dreams come true for many prospective homeowners. Rita, his partner and helpmate, enjoys gardening, crafting, and loving their dogs, past and present.

James and Helen Henry had two daughters, Nancy and Susan, and one granddaughter, Tina, who completed their schooling in Middlesex. Helen taught first grade for 25 years from 1951 through 1976 at Pierce, Watchung, and Von E. Mauger Schools. James served as a volunteer fireman for over 50 years and worked as a funeral director at Taggart Chamberlain Funeral Home.

Dorothy G. Horst, who passed away in 2007, was well loved by her children Lon H. Balunis and Gordon Horst, grandchildren, and great-grandchildren Bryan, Jennifer, Kyle, and Katelyn. Dorothy was president of the Middlesex Band Booster Club and the Middlesex Borough Alliance Committee. Gordon has been a member of the Middlesex Elks and is on the board of trustees.

Pictured here are, from left to right, David, Robert, Gary, Paul, and Stephen Fisk, the children of Clyde and Priscilla Fisk. Paul and Stephen carry on in their father's tradition and operate Fisk Associates, the surveying and engineering offices at the corner of Route 28 and Orchard Road. The Fisk name has stood for quality workmanship for over two generations, and this family has provided service with class and dignity.

Phyllis and Walter Durniak have lived in Middlesex for 47 years. Their sons Jeff (right) and Chris graduated from Middlesex High School. Jeff, a biologist, lives in Georgia with his wife, Karen. Chris, a naturalist, and his wife, Karen, have traveled extensively, returning each year to Indonesia to visit the many friends they have made in remote villages.

Alex and Barbara Morecraft are seen here enjoying the beach at Cape May in 2003. Alex was born in Middlesex and graduated from Bound Brook High School and Lafayette College. He served in the army in Korea and Georgia. After leaving the army, he became a teacher and coach at Middlesex High School for 30 years. Barbara and Alex have two sons, Michael and Kenneth, and have lived in the same house on Louis Avenue for 40 years.

Robert and Patricia Martin are pictured with their two children, Denise Martin and Bob Martin. Robert worked in Newark as a longshoreman, and Patricia worked with children at a day care school and as a legal secretary. Denise and Bob both graduated from Middlesex High School. Denise is a legal secretary, and Bob works for Chubb Insurance Company.

Enjoying a holiday dinner in 1993 are, from left to right, Marge Hanania, her daughter Laura, grandchildren Eric and Brian Matland, and her husband, Hal. Marge was hired as secretary to the borough clerk in 1962, was appointed as borough clerk in 1973, and became clerk/administrator in 1977. She retired in 1987. Hal organized the Middlesex Borough Horseshoe Club in 1964 and served as a police officer here from 1955 until he retired as a captain in 1981.

This picture of the Kirk family was taken in Mountainview Park in Middlesex. Granddaughter Karolyn Kirk is in front. Standing proudly behind her are, from left to right, (first row) grandsons Alexander and Aidan Fromme; (second row) Carol Kirk, her daughter Karen Fromme, and Carol's husband, Elmer Kirk. Carol moved to Middlesex from Jersey City with her mother, Mrs. Cooney, and her sisters.

Leshanda "Mae" Pitt, also known as "Lossie" and as "Mother Pitt" by her fellow churchgoers, worked in the cotton fields of North Carolina as a child. She moved to Middlesex and has become a local legend. Pitt is a certified home-health aide. She cares for the ill and elderly, cooks holiday meals for those confined to their homes on Thanksgiving and Christmas, and finds clothing and furniture for families in need.

Dan and Irmgard Nebb owned the house at 205 Ashland Road, which they purchased in 1943. They raised their five daughters here in Middlesex, and all the girls attended local schools and graduated from Middlesex High School. The girls are Shirley, Jane, Judy, Louise, and Patricia.

In 1969, the Vincent Tagliaferro family was a young family in a young neighborhood. Children Anthony and Maureen, dressed in their Sunday best, pose for a picture with their father on the front lawn of their home on Ambrose Avenue. The Ambrose Avenue neighborhood was a relatively new neighborhood in the 1960s.

Earl DeSiato, age nine, starts his career as a hydroplane racer in 1968 in Lakewood in a boat named *Go-Go* built by his father, Oreste "Rusty" DeSiato. The DeSiato family members all became avid boat racers and have won medals and trophies in races throughout the United States. Louise DeSiato, Oreste's wife, has always been the family's chief fan and supporter.

The eight-foot Christmas tree, which is decorated with lights, ornaments, and garland and topped with an angel, dwarfs Anna Bitow. This is a typical Christmas scene in Middlesex. Anna Bitow moved to Middlesex on New Year's Eve in 1950 with her husband, Steve. She is shown here celebrating her 58th year as a resident of Middlesex Borough. Steve was a member of the board of education for many years.

Walter Paul Sr. is pictured here at his home on Second Street with his son, Walter Jr. Walter Sr. was originally from Hoboken, where he lived next door to Frank Sinatra. He met his wife, Helen, at a dance in South Plainfield, where he attended school. He worked at the Plainfield Post Office for many years.

Young Christine Polakiewicz smiles for the camera. Christine is the granddaughter of the late Thaddeus (Ted) Polakiewicz and his wife, Irene. Ted was an active member of the H. C. Pierce Hose Company for several decades. Irene still resides in her longtime home on C Street.

Teri Hoski and her husband, Joe, came to Middlesex from Jersey City in 1954. They purchased a flower shop in the Middlesex Shopping Center from the Boehme family. The Hoskis operated the shop until their retirement, at which time their daughter Renee took responsibility for the business. During holiday seasons, the whole family joined together to insure that all the work got done properly. Pictured here in front of the store are three generations, grandson Dean Hoski, daughter Renee, and parents Teri and Joe.

Maria Renda is a typical proud grandmother with two little grandsons. Pictures such as these are commonly taken in this town. They reflect what happens throughout the borough, loving families living together, working and growing together. These children benefit from the love, support, and knowledge passed down to them from past generations.

Summer is a great time for family picnics, and these youngsters are taking a break from eating hot dogs and hamburgers to pose for the camera. They are eager to continue to play games and enjoy their afternoon. Family backyard picnics are a favorite form of entertainment in Middlesex.

Mohamed and Alba Sadaty smile for the camera in front of their Middlesex home in 1977. Mohamed, a beloved pediatrician, and Alba, his wife and nurse assistant, cared for most Middlesex children in the 1970s and 1980s, bringing them safely through their infancy, toddler years, preteens, and adolescence. An extremely dedicated team, they were missed by the community when they retired to Florida. Mohamed continues to volunteer his services and is currently writing a medical book.

From left to right, Honna and Col. Michael Kozik Jr. and Elfi and Michael Kozik are attending a Marine Corps ball in Johnstown, Pennsylvania. The colonel served two tours of duty in Iraq as a harrier pilot and is now a reserve officer and a commercial pilot for American Airlines. His father, Michael, was a volunteer fireman for Middlesex and former chief of the fire department. He served as the third vice commander of the American Legion Post 306.

A Halloween costume party is a time for fun, food, and costumes. Karen Mason is enjoying the occasion with Jiggs the schnauzer looking on. Mason left Middlesex to study in Oregon. Today she is deeply involved in Christian ministry through signing for the deaf. Her parents, Joan and George Mason of Hazelwood Avenue, also answered the call of the West and reside today in sunny California.

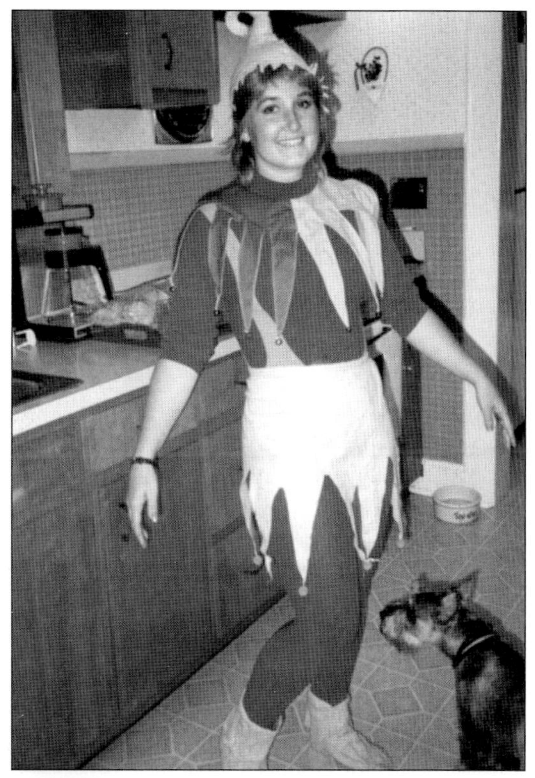

Bonnie and Cindy seem to be standing at attention as Rita Lopa (left) and a friend watch. Maybe the dogs see a bird or a lovely butterfly. Most certainly, there is no danger lurking, or the girls would be ferociously guarding their humans. How beautiful and proud they are.

Robert and Elsie Nelson lived in Middlesex since the mid-1950s. All their children attended the public schools. Pictured here are Elsie and Robert with, from left to right, sons Eric, Christian, and Jeffrey. Their daughter Dr. Lisa Kelchner lives with her family in Ohio. Elsie was known for her children's programs at the Middlesex Public Library, especially for her original puppet shows starring lovable Rufus. She continued Marion McCreary's column, "Middlesex Day by Day," for the *Middlesex Chronicle*.

Andrew and Robin Galida are pictured here with their two children, Andrew, age 13, and Eric, age 10. The elder Andrew lived in Middlesex since 1964 with his parents, Andrew and Margaret Galida. He attended Middlesex schools, and when he married Robin, they moved to Orchard Road. He is a partner in a company doing commercial environmental cleanup. Like most parents, the Galidas are happily involved with their sons' sports activities.

One would hardly think that two lawyers, one engineer, and a special education teacher would be clowning around like this. Sibling rivalry never dies, as evidenced by the Johnson family. In front are, from left to right, Greg, Steve, and Paul. Behind her brothers is Jenny. It is Christmas and a good time for families to be together.

Pictured here are the three children of Peter and Edythe Staffelli. On the left is John, who served 16 years in the U. S. Navy, becoming a petty officer first class. John had four sons. In the middle is Edie Fritzinger, proud mom to lovely Jessica. Edie is a graduate of Endicott College with a degree in business. She is currently employed by Sodexo USA. On the right is Peter Jr., a graduate of Seton Hall University and employed by International Coach Parts, Inc. Peter is a dad to two beautiful daughters.

Jack Van Doren, who died in 2007, was one of the members of the Middlesex Borough Heritage Committee. He is pictured here, relaxing in his chair in his front yard on Father's Day in 2003. He is surrounded by his family, including his wife, Marilyn; daughter, Tracey; grandchildren Nancy and Neil; and son, Lloyd. Jack's enthusiasm, ideas, and friendship are greatly missed by the committee.

The Canavan family has given much to the borough in public service. Bob Canavan is an active member of Our Lady of Mount Virgin Roman Catholic Church and also of the local chapter of the Ancient Order of Hibernians as well as a past president of the Middlesex Borough Rescue Squad. His wife, Kathy, is an avid quilter and homemaker. Pictured are, from left to right, their seven children, Kathleen Canavan Truskoroski, Michael Canavan, Eileen Canavan McCarthy, Mary Beth Canavan, Tom Canavan, Bob Canavan, and John Canavan.

Six

Serving Town and Country

John R. Staffelli, the son of Peter and Edythe, was a proud grandson of former mayor Louis Staffelli. A happy and personable young man and anxious to follow family tradition in food service, John attended Johnson and Wales University, aspiring to be a master chef. Then answering his country's call, John joined the navy, and during his career, he became a chef for Gen. Colin Powell. He served for 16 years, attaining the rank of petty officer first class.

What is an American?

Kaitlyn Anthony Grade 5 Von E Mauger

An American is a happy, free, honest, hard working, and independent person. As Americans, we are given many freedoms. Along with our freedom comes responsibility. Two qualities that I feel are most important in an American are good citizenship and loyalty.

In order for a person to be a good citizen, they must want and work to make America a better place for everyone to live. For example, there is a man who comes to our local library every week to collect food for F.I.S.H., an organization which collects food for the needy. I think that he is a great example of a good citizen. That's one of the most important qualities to me as an American.

Being loyal to America means that you respect it and will go to all limits to keep it and the people in it safe. I still cannot believe how brave those men and women were in that horrible time of 9-11. They risked their lives just to protect fellow Americans. These people are a really good example of great Americans.

What is an American? An American is a loyal person and a good citizen. Being free is just one of our many right rights. Consider yourself lucky to be an American.

Kaitlyn Anthony, as a sixth grader at Von E. Mauger School, expresses her feelings about America so eloquently that it makes one proud of today's youth. An all-American girl, Anthony loves Girl Scouts, tap dancing, fishing, Sunday school, and many other interests. In her essay, she pays tribute to Ralph Magliette, a library board member who collects food for FISH at the library.

Mayor Martin Matuszkiewicz has just delivered a short talk to the Middlesex Boy and Girl Scouts at the Lincoln memorial located at the corner of Lincoln Boulevard and Mountain Avenue. Every year, the borough celebrates Pres. Abraham Lincoln's birthday in February by having a ceremony at the site of the Lincoln statue in town. This year, there was a little snow on the ground.

Veterans of Foreign Wars commander Vincent Tagliaferro appears on the left in this photograph with senior vice commander Joe Vaccaro on the right placing wreaths during a town Memorial Day celebration. The Lincoln statue is in the background. Both men were World War II veterans and lived in Middlesex Borough for many years. They both served multiple terms in their official positions in Veterans of Foreign Wars Post 6988.

Beverly Weber has been a member of the Middlesex Public Library Board of Trustees since 1985 and served as its president for four years during the construction of the library expansion. The new community room in the expanded library was named in her honor. As leader of the Friends of the Library, she has provided Middlesex citizens with numerous educational, entertaining, and cultural programs. Weber is an accomplished musician, a tireless worker, a worthy protagonist, and a good and loyal friend to all who know her.

The Middlesex Fire Department Ladies Auxiliary gathers by the side of the Lincoln firehouse prior to one of the borough's parades in the early 1970s. The auxiliary helps to support many of the functions of the fire department and assists at parties and celebrations. It also helps to raise money to support the volunteer fire department.

Students from the high school get a chance to act as mayor, borough clerk, borough attorney, and council members while conducting an actual meeting of the governing body. Paired in 1972 are, from left to right, council member Franklin Kistner with Greg Kubliska, council member Jack Walsh with Dave Agans, council member Frank Santangelo with Janet Matts, attorney Bill Gazi with Wayne Fredrickson, Mayor Martin Matuskiewicz with Larry McBride, borough clerk Elmer Hoagland with Harry Kochler, council member Ed Massessa with Ellen Boyd, council member Michael Feldman with Kevin Dickey, and council member Robert Jarechi with Bonnie Hawk.

Pictured here receiving flu shots are Mayor Walter Rafferty and members of the 1960 borough council, from left to right, Walter Ryan, Harold Jahnke, Everitt Landers, George Gould, Louis Curcio, and William Howes. During this council's tenure, in 1960, radioactive material was discovered at the borough's dump site, and Hurricane Donna caused severe flooding damage throughout the borough. In 1961, the council received the request to use the old borough hall building as a library.

Phil Ackerman, smiling on the right, is congratulated by local resident Charles Semmer for recognition he received as president of the New Jersey Central First Aid Council during the years 1991 to 1993. He joined the local rescue squad in 1957, winning awards for heroism, delivering nine babies, and serving in executive positions on the Middlesex squad and the State of New Jersey first aid councils.

Bill Engelman and Martin Matuszkiewicz stand in front of the firemen's memorial during one of the many parades held in the borough. Matuszkiewicz was mayor of the borough from 1970 to 1980 as well as a former fire chief. Engelman was head of the office of emergency management for many years as well as having been a former fire chief.

Thomas Edward Gorman, a Bayonne native, was a resident of Middlesex along with his family on September 11, 2001. He died that fateful day as a hero responding to the call of duty at the Twin Towers inferno. He was a member of the emergency service unit of the New York-New Jersey Port Authority Police. Hundreds attended a special memorial service held for him at Our Lady of Mount Virgin Roman Catholic Church. His wife, Barbara, and their children, Bridget, Laura, and Patrick, still reside in the community.

Members of the H. C. Pierce Hose Company and the ladies auxiliary pose for a group picture in 1966. From left to right are (first row) Dorothy Ferrand, Agnes Wyckoff, Jean Ross, Bee Vanderhoof, George Senna, Joe Leccese, Andy Persinko, Glenn Anderson, Ken Wyckoff, and John Ross; (second row) Evie Schofield, unidentified, Lana Gerster, Louie Ferrand, Ted Polakiewicz, Henry Perrine, George Schaub, Ralph Nye, Jim Powers, and Ed Vanderhoof; (third row) unidentified, Vi Schaub, Irene Polakiewicz, Bill Johnson, Tony Staffieri, Hans Gerster, Howie Ames, Hans Wagner, Lou Conrad, Chuck Sobotka, and Frank Taylor.

The police monument, now located in front of the new police headquarters building on Mountain Avenue, was dedicated on September 16, 1989. The monument was designed to honor the professional police officers of the borough. The members of the monument committee who met over a two-year period resulting in this beautiful tribute were chairman Edward King, police chief Sylvester Conrad, Mayor Ronald Dobies, Adam Bubrow, Cynthia A. Chomen, Peter J. Diskin, municipal court judge George L. Psak, Walter Rajca, and J. V. Tavaglione.

This group of elementary students poses respectfully in front of a large paper birthday cake with 200 candles during America's bicentennial year in 1976, commemorating the birth of the nation. The year 1976 was a most festive year, with ceremonies and activities taking place on the national, state, and local levels.

Middlesex Borough's September 11 monument, measuring 9 feet 11 inches high, was erected on October 23, 2004, at the entrance to Victor Crowell Park. The multicolor river rocks of varying sizes that surround the base represent the diversity of those who lost their lives when the Twin Towers collapsed. The two missing stripes in the center of the flag represent the two World Trade Center towers and the gap created by the loss of so many lives.

In 1966, the H. C. Pierce Hose Company No. 1 had this fire truck as engine No. 3 of the Middlesex Fire Department. The borough has four separate fire companies. Pierce was founded by Hugh C. Pierce, who was one of the original developers of the borough. The officers pictured here are, from left to right, George Senna, Joe Leccese, Harry Perrine, and Chief George Schaub.

John Fuhrmann was president of the Middlesex Borough Jaycees, and he subsequently served on the borough planning board for 3 years, on the zoning board for 12 years, and on the borough council for 9 years. He was instrumental in getting approval for the borough's senior citizen housing complex. He has also served as master of ceremonies at many municipal functions, including the borough's bicentennial celebration in 1976.

Sheila Fuhrmann served for several years as a member of the Middlesex Borough Zoning Board and the Middlesex Borough Board of Education. She was active in the Middlesex League of Women Voters, serving as president for a term. She is probably best known, however, as the director of the borough's department of aging. She is loved and respected by her many senior citizen clients because of her skill, knowledge, and compassion in dealing with their problems.

Natalie Jesionka is an independent filmmaker and media literacy advocate. Over the last few years, she has worked closely with Amnesty International and United Nations Educational, Scientific and Cultural Organization (UNESCO) to promote global human rights through media and film. She has produced documentaries about illegal immigration, human trafficking, and gender discrimination throughout the world. She is the executive director for the Prizm Project, a nonprofit group that promotes young women's human rights education.

In 2007, the Middlesex Friends of the Library hosted an afternoon of remembering the "old days" in Middlesex. Among others, Peter Staffelli, lifetime resident and son of former mayor Louis Staffelli, shares stories with former mayors Ronald Dobies and Joseph Zuccarelli. Other panelists, as well, took turns telling tales of trolley lines, corner stores, sites long since disappeared, and people and ideas that shaped Middlesex Borough. A good time was had by all, participants and observers alike.

Richard Pachucki served as exalted ruler of the Middlesex Borough Elks Lodge and was the owner of Boro Hall Pharmacy in Middlesex for many years. He recently retired and sold his business, but the new owner carries on the tradition of friendly and courteous service that was maintained by Pachucki.

Nick Lance, right, graduated from Middlesex High School in 1968 and Georgia Institute of Technology in 1973 with a degree in mechanical engineering. In 1968, he started working for NASA while still in college. He participated in the Apollo Program, the Apollo-Soyuz Test Project, the space shuttle, and the International Space Station. Currently he is on the staff of the director of engineering at Johnson Space Center.

In May 1971, a large group of students and teachers from Our Lady of Mount Virgin School took a class trip to Washington, D.C. A small group of them are shown here on the Capitol steps with U.S. congressman Edward Patten. From left to right are Denise Breiner, Cathyann Conrad, Sr. Mary Joseph, Patten, Roseanne Kosloski, and Edward Fenty.

Gregory Creighton is taking instruction from fireman Robert Ring very seriously during Fire Prevention Week in 1991. This community event is held in October each year to promote and guarantee the safety of the residents, students, and businesses in Middlesex.

Sherley Penrose has been a dedicated volunteer whose service to the community has been appreciated by all. She has been active in Girl Scouting for years. She has served as a borough council member and a member of the Middlesex Borough Recreation Commission, borough beautification committee, and hometown committee. Penrose still has time to enjoy her roles as wife, mother, and grandmother.

Dr. Zafar Shaheen was born in Mysore in southern India. He interned at Albert Einstein Medical Center and completed residencies in internal medicine and cardiology at Catholic Medical Center in New York and Robert Wood Johnson Medical School. He opened his medical office in Middlesex in 1982 and is beloved by his patients. He is a humanitarian who truly cares for all his patients.

The Memorial Day celebration, which has been an annual affair in town, continues to realize excellent support from all citizens. This photograph, which was taken in 1986, shows two outstanding Middlesex volunteers. On the left is Walter Rajca, owner of the Middlesex Funeral Home, and on the right is Robert Agans, who was a captain in the Middlesex Police Department.

Rich Pachucki and Monique Sasso celebrate the arrival of the year 1984 in front of the Sasso home on Giles Avenue. Sasso and her husband, Tony, hold an annual "dropping of the ball," Times Square style, on their front lawn. Pachucki was the longtime owner of Boro Hall Pharmacy and is an active in the local and state Elks organization. Sasso is an active leader in the local Ladies Elks.

Ronald Dobies served as mayor of Middlesex from 1980 to 2005, and prior to serving as mayor, he was a member and president of the Middlesex Board of Education. Dobies is a chemist and worked for years overseeing research projects for American Cyanimid Company. For many years, he commuted from Middlesex to Pearl River, New York, and yet still found time to put in an average 20 hours each week doing borough business.

Lt. Gen. Norman Seip graduated from Middlesex High School in 1970, the United States Air Force Academy in 1974, and Air War College in 1994. In his career, he has logged over 4,500 hours in fighter aircraft, primarily FI5E. He was deputy air component commander in Operation Iraqi Freedom, Operation Enduring Freedom, and Joint Task Force Horn of Africa. He is presently commander of the 12th Air Force and Air Forces Southern at Davis-Monthan Air Force Base in Arizona.

John (Jack) Walsh served on the Middlesex Borough Council in the early 1970s during the administration of Mayor Martin Matuszkiewicz. He helped in the welcoming of many people who participated in the World Horseshoe Tournament that was held in Mountainview Park in Middlesex during the summer of 1971. His wife, Rosemary Walsh, has served for many years as a member and former president of the Middlesex Board of Education.

Msgr. William J. Haughney served as pastor of Our Lady of Mount Virgin Roman Catholic Church from 1983 to 1996. A graduate of Seton Hall University, he completed his studies for the priesthood at Immaculate Conception Seminary in Darlington. Later he obtained a master of sacred theology degree at Princeton Theological Seminary. He was ordained as a priest on May 31, 1947. He retired in 1996 but continues to serve by celebrating mass in Middlesex, Bound Brook, and South Bound Brook.

Jack DeAngelis and his brother Frank DeAngelis both served in the navy during World War II. They were on different ships, and two of the ships on which Jack served were sunk by Japanese torpedoes. After the war, Jack started his own contracting business and Frank joined him. They built several hundred homes in Middlesex and the surrounding area. Frank retired from building in 1975, but Jack is still plying his trade today.

For many years, Frank DeAngelis served as chairman of the Middlesex Borough Planning Board. After retiring, he dedicated his life to helping and honoring veterans and their families by making over 1,000 shadow boxes and donating them to veterans or their families. These boxes were used to display the many medals and ribbons won by the veterans during their military service. For his service to the military, DeAngelis is the only person who has been made an honorary member of both the Band of Brothers (E Company, 506th Parachute Infantry Regiment, U.S. Army 101st Airborne Division) and the Tuskegee Airmen.

Mayor Gerald D'Angelo and the Middlesex Borough Council are pictured during one of their Tuesday evening meetings. The governing body has regular meetings on the second and fourth Tuesday of the month. Pictured from left to right are (first row) Robert Schuler, Mayor Gerald D'Angelo, and Michael Venuto; (second row) Robert Gore, Kenneth DeVuyst, Kathleen Anello (borough clerk), Sean Kaplan, and Robert Edwards.

Edward Winters has been a volunteer fireman in Middlesex Borough for 41 years. He served as fire chief in 1970 and 1980, and he was elected again in 2005, 2006, 2007, and 2008. As chief of the fire department, he is liaison with the mayor and council and keeps the local governing body abreast of all the activities of the department.

In September 1992, thanks mainly to the efforts of chairman John Fuhrmann and the Middlesex Senior Citizens' Housing Committee, the borough obtained a federal grant of $6.75 million to construct a senior citizens' building to provide affordable housing for elderly residents on fixed incomes. Members of the committee are pictured here at the groundbreaking ceremony together with representatives from the construction company and the management company.

In 1994, Middlesex Borough's first and only senior citizens' housing project, known as Watchung Terrace, was completed. This five-story, 86-unit complex provides affordable housing to senior citizens. Rents are adjusted based on the income of the resident, and as a result of an annual federal grant, the federal government pays the difference between what the resident can afford and the market rental for the unit.

CPSIA information can be obtained at www.ICGtesting.com
Printed in the USA
BVOW07s0916100414

350222BV00004B/11/P

9 781624 195402

This Place That I Go...

True Accounts of. . .
Angels, Blessings, Dreams,
Visions, Ministering Spirits, and End of Life Experiences

GLENDA SMITH WALTERS

This Place That I Go. . .
by Glenda Smith Walters

Printed in the United States of America

ISBN 9781624195402

 A portion of the proceeds will go towards Hospice care. Through the purchases of the parable, "I Am the Deep Blue Ocean," a portion of the proceeds will go to the Sea Turtle Protection Project, conducted in Oak Island, North Carolina.

Front cover artwork - Abbott Handerson Thayer, American, 1849-1921, Winged Figure, 1889, Oil on canvas, 130.8 x 95.9 cm (51 1/2 x 37 3/4 in.), Simeon B. Williams Fund, 1947.32, The Art Institute of Chicago. Photography © The Art Institute of Chicago.

Back cover photo, and photos within book – courtesy of Mike Melton, P.O. Box 61885, North Charleston, SC. Photography © G. Mike Melton.

Bible quotations are taken from the King James Version of the Bible.

The stories are true, but names, places, and other identifying details have been changed for those individuals who wish to remain anonymous. If any incidents described in this book seem familiar, it is due to the fact that many of these same scenarios, concerning spiritual experiences occur frequently at the end of life.

Xulon Press
www.xulonpress.com

Printed in the United States of America
First Edition: October 2012

Blessings,

Glenda A. Walters

DEDICATION

Rochella Baker
10/12/35 – 1/15/03

This book is dedicated to my dear friend, Rochella Baker. She was one of the most courageous women I've ever known, having battled Lou Gehrig's disease for over eighteen years. I regret that she is not here to see that I followed through on a project that was started over 15 years ago. I hope that somehow she knows that her many pep talks finally paid off. Here's to you Rochella, for your giving spirit, and for planting a seed of hope within me, of what could be if we do not give up on our dreams. You taught me that if I believe, then something incredible happens ...my mind is open to this place that I go.

CONTENTS

"The most beautiful thing we can experience is the mysterious. It is the source of all true art and science. He to whom this emotion is a stranger, who can no longer pause to wonder and stand rapt in awe, is as good as dead: his eyes are closed."

. . .Albert Einstein[1]

ACKNOWLEDGEMENTS

This book could not have been written without the help of the individuals I met along the way, who bravely shared their heart-felt stories. Many thanks go out to Marilyn and Jim McAfee, for giving me a key to their home when I first embarked on this adventure. It came with an invitation to use their computer at any given time. When this project was started I did not own one. I will always be grateful for their kindness. Thanks to Marilyn McAfee, Ann Wilcox, Judy Dunaway and Mike Melton for assistance with proofing and editing. Thanks to Mike Melton, providing the graphics (other than the front cover) throughout the book. For info on the graphics, you may contact him at meltong@triad.rr.com.

My gratitude goes out to my good friend, Coralyn "Anastasia" Theodoridis for understanding that I needed to write this on my own. I wish to give credit to my angel author friend Leonard Day (deceased), Hospice volunteers Betty Brown, Robert and Ramona Phelps, Cleo Tulburt (deceased), and my friends C.B. Tatum, Crystal Troutman, Rosemary Russell (deceased), Tonya Ragan, Winoka Plummer, Vickey Crotts, Crystal Wickham, Polly Spainhour, Lloyd Rawson, Beverly Blythe, and Sandra Hughes. These individuals each played a part in providing the wind beneath my wings through our many talks along the way.

I wish to thank Reverend Richard Cockman, formerly with Faith Alliance Church of Midway, North Carolina. He reminded me that if God had led me to my prior position with Hospice of Davidson County, then he would calm my fears and give me the inner strength needed to perform my duties. I would have missed a wonderful chapter in my life had it not been for his wisdom and reassurance.

PREFACE

What you're about to read may be unbelievable, especially for those who do not acknowledge that another world exists. The world that I'm referring to resides within another dimension. Let me assure you that the stories within these pages are true.

In my mid-twenties a new realm began opening up for me, one that was often unnerving. Visions and dreams foretold future events, spirits unknown and known to me paid visits in the middle of the night, and messages were given ahead of time. For years I shared these accounts with only a few close friends for fear of what people would think.

However, we have reached an age when many individuals are opening their minds to the possibility that a spirit world could co-exist with ours. After all, God is a spirit and therefore he dwells and works each day within this same spiritual realm. We each have our beliefs, and I respect that fact. My hope is that you will keep an open mind as you travel through the pages of these recorded stories.

It was not until my forties that my passion for writing surfaced. Leonard Day (deceased), a High Point, North Carolina author asked me to submit articles for a publication known as Direct Pathways. Leonard wrote for this same newsletter, published by Suzanne King Herndon (deceased,) and printed by a High Point newspaper. It was distributed to over 400 churches and organizations within the Triad. After four years of writing for this publication, I wanted to know if my articles were making a difference.

One morning, on my way to work I decided to pray for the answer. That very afternoon I received a call at 2 p.m. from a woman named Cheryl. She introduced herself and began

thanking me, explaining how one of my stories had saved her life. She shared that her husband had left her for someone else, leaving her with only $2.00 in her wallet, no car, and a run-down house. As if this were not enough, she had recently been diagnosed with a brain tumor. Cheryl stated that she had risen at 4 a.m. that morning, walked into her bathroom fully intending to end her life with a prescription of pain medicine.

As she picked up the pills she noticed a Direct Pathways newsletter lying face up on the floor, opened to my column. With each issue the publication ran our photos along with our stories. Cheryl went on to say, “Ms. Walters, there was something about your eyes, they looked right into my soul. After reading your story about your great-grandfather (“A Request Granted”) I decided that there was something left to live for.”

My prayer had been answered in a matter of hours through a woman named Cheryl. I had been given proof that God was using these stories, like so many other stories throughout the world to touch the lives of others. In other words, it’s not about me. Like you, I’m merely one of many instruments that God works through. With the help of Hospice volunteers and local churches we raised enough donations to purchase Cheryl a used vehicle, acquired donated furniture, and much-needed funds. The last time we spoke she sounded happy and full of hope.

Within these pages are a collection of spiritual events, not only from a Hospice perspective, but from the experiences of people from all walks of life. It is overflowing with angels and near-death experiences, blessings, answered prayers, visions and dreams, while acknowledging that the dark side does exist. This book opens one’s eyes to everyday miracles, and that Heaven and Hell are for real.

These stories challenge the reader to explore what is possible if you just believe. It opens our minds to the belief that we can live our lives as if every day produces miracles. Albert Einstein once stated, “there are only two ways to live your life. One is as though nothing is a miracle. The other is as though everything is a miracle.” [1.]

Although, we are living in turbulent times, we are also living in a period of a great awakening. Within the last twenty-some years it seems that God is trying to wake us up. He appears to be putting forth his own plan to gain our attention... before it’s too late. The PAX television channel has aired such hit shows

as, "Touched by an Angel"[2] and "It's A Miracle."[3] These shows bolstered our faith and showed us that there is a connection between angels, miracles, and man. A show called, "Joan of Arcadia," portrayed Amber Tamblyn as Joan, a teen that God spoke to.[4] Guideposts began publishing an additional magazine, known as "Angels on Earth."

There was a time when mysterious billboards were springing up across our nation with slogans like, "don't make me come down there," "let's talk," or "let's meet at my house Sunday before the game," all signed by God." The actor Mel Gibson produced "The Passion of the Christ," a movie that impacted over 500 million people.[5]

More recently, my niece and I enjoyed watching reruns of "The Ghost Whisperer."[6] This series was about a young woman who owned an antique shop, and could see spirits who had chosen not to walk into the light. In this now cancelled show, Jennifer Love Hewitt played the part of Melinda. Her role was to encourage those who had passed away... who were trapped between two worlds, to cross over.

The popular radio station, known as "K-Love," 97.3 continues to grow their listening base each day by uplifting those who need hope. They speak daily words of faith, and play recordings of popular spirit-filled artists. Motivational speakers, such as Rev. Joel Osteen, and Dr. Wayne W. Dyer plant seeds of encouragement through their many books and programmed shows. It's my belief that God did not stop writing after he produced the Bible. Over the centuries, and even today God continues to inspire individuals to produce, direct, write, or speak messages that help us grow our faith.

In this fast paced world that we live in, where we rarely slow down long enough to enjoy the stillness of the moment, could God be using his own strategy...his own plan to gain our attention? Remember the verse, "Be still and know that I am God?" How often do we take the time to sit down and give him a moment? After the events of September 11, 2001, unemployment, the recession, and the fact that the baby boomers have reached an age of reflection... these events have caused many of us to review our lives.

Numerous individuals have opted for a more meaningful career, to work for themselves, and to live a simpler lifestyle. These same individuals are searching for spiritual truths, along

with what they should be doing with their lives. Many individuals are looking for a way out of Corporate America. They find that they must take their work home each day in order to keep up the pace, thus keeping them from quality time with their family and friends. Not only are they exhausted, carrying the load of two and three people in the workplace, but many workers are saddened to know that they are no longer valued by management. In some cases they soon find that they are merely a number that can easily be erased.

The way we were raised, the church we attend, the social environment we choose to live in, the books we read, and the programs we watch, all play a part in a belief system that has been formed over time. Laurie Beth Jones summed it up best in her book, "The Power of Positive Prophecy." She drives home the statement, "cultural conditioning tells us what we believe, and thus dictates how we behave."[7]

When I took on the role of Volunteer Coordinator for Hospice of Davidson County, one of our patient volunteers stated, "Angels and miracles do not exist today... they only took place in biblical times." This older gentleman was a devout deacon in his church, so what made him make such a profound statement? Throughout his life, his religious teachings had shaped his belief system... thus an example of "cultural conditioning." The Bible states that God never changes. It is man that brings about change through his own religious rituals and his own written words. Our human side tends to view everything in the physical instead of the spiritual. By nature, we wish to come up with a logical, scientific answer for an encounter... a visitation from the other side that we cannot explain.

In her book "Messages," Bonnie McEneaney shares accounts of signs, visits, and premonitions from loved ones who lost their lives on 9/11.[8] Through her interviews she learned that many of the victims, who had worked in the Twin Towers experienced dreams and strong feelings, that something was about to take place before that fateful day. Later, the spouses and friends of those who died on 9/11 told of seeing their loved ones and friends in their dreams, while others experienced visitations. The author admitted to being a skeptic on spiritual matters before losing her husband on that tragic day. When Eamon, her deceased husband began sending her and his friends signs and messages she had no choice but to believe.

There are those who have come to believe that there is the possibility that we knew one another... within our inner circle here, before we came into this world. It is their theory that we were meant to forget what we knew before we were born in order to concentrate on our lessons... our missions here. Many individuals who encountered a near-death experience have stated later that they were told by God or Jesus that they would not be able to remember the conversations that took place while in heaven, that there was a reason for this. Those individuals that theorize we knew one another before our birth believe that God created the spirit first. Therefore, individuals who played, or now play a role in our lives could possibly have known us before we were born here.

If our spirit was created first, what if we were known as that spirit before being placed in our mother's womb? Jeremiah 1:5 states; *"Before I formed thee in the belly I knew thee: and before thou camest forth out of the womb I sanctified thee."* In this verse, one could interpret that God is revealing to us that he created our spirit first. He then placed us in our mother's womb and blessed us. Of course, we will not have all the answers until we arrive in Heaven.

Some would have you believe in Heaven and not Hell... in angels, but not demons. Yet, for some Hospice patients and individuals who died and were later revived, they shared with me that they were shown both Hell and Heaven when they crossed over. These same individuals stated that they encountered angels and dark spirits when they traveled through the tunnel to the other side. However, others shared that they traveled straight to the light, never experiencing the dark side.

It is my wish that the words within these pages heal old wounds, uplift those who are depressed, and give renewed strength to those who have lost all hope. May it bring closure to those who have lost loved ones, and may it provide proof that our spirits do live on once we die. It was written for you to take something from it... to assure you that your own supernatural encounters and dream-like "visitations" could be for real.

I do hope that as you read these remarkable stories, your mind will be open to the belief that there is an afterlife, both good and bad.

HISTORY OF HOSPICE

The word "Hospice" stands for "a place of rest." It was derived from the word "hostel," a place where long ago weary travelers bedded down for the night. In 1967 a physician, known as Dr. Cicely Saunders founded the first Hospice in London, England. Hospice came over to the United States in the 70's. Mother Teresa also established Hospices throughout the world. She founded the Missionaries of Charity, a Roman Catholic religious congregation, which consists of over 4,500 nuns, and active in 133 countries.

The Hospice team comes into your home, or into a skilled nursing facility to create an environment of comfort to meet the medical needs of the enrolled patient that is terminally ill. At Hospice we take into account that the mental, spiritual, and physical needs are met, while respecting the patient's and caregiver's wishes. One does not have to wait until the last days of someone's life to make a referral to Hospice. A doctor must sign that one has 6 months or less. We have had patients in the Hospice program for more than six months, but they must continue to show signs of decline in order to stay within the Medicare guidelines.

Hospice can provide respite for the caregiver by way of a volunteer, cover the cost of most prescribed medications, provide nurses to monitor their condition, and aides to bathe and provide hygiene care. Having Hospice in any given setting, is like having a second pair of eyes... to discover conditions that others may not see early on.

INTRODUCTION

For I know the thoughts that I think toward you, saith the LORD, thoughts of peace, and not of evil, to give you an expected end.

...Jeremiah 29:11

Before taking a position at Hospice I worked for a furniture-based mail order firm. We were a close-knit group who socialized outside of the office as well. There were parties, family picnics, and a company softball team. After five years our staff tripled in size and a more aggressive sales staff was added. The family camaraderie we once shared as a smaller group disappeared. Unfortunately, the atmosphere changed to a more competitive one.

My last position within the company involved working in product development, creating a furniture line around a famous actor. Although my job was exciting, it came with twelve-hour days and lots of deadlines. I longed for a job with fewer hours, one that would make a difference within my community. It may not have been a good idea for me to have bartered with God. However, I found myself promising that in exchange for the job I longed for, I would volunteer for a local non-profit organization.

Almost a year had passed since making that promise, when one night, as I sat up in bed reading my bible I somehow knew my prayers would be answered soon. Upon knowing this, it was important for me to leave a message behind. Part of my job consisted of contributing copy for the company newsletter. I wanted to write a piece that would motivate the staff to consider changing their course.

It was at that moment an unseen entity sat down on my bed and leaned against my feet. After thinking back on this moment, that took place so long ago I'm convinced that this was an angel, who had come to give me the message that I had requested.

Words began to flow so swiftly through my mind that I had no choice but to race to the den to retrieve a pad and pen. The following parable was given to me on that night some nineteen years ago. It ran in the company newsletter one week before I was laid off:

Life's Many Plays

Life is like a series of plays. We all have been given our parts. It is how we play our part that matters. If we act so that we support one another, then the play is beautifully done... we bring the house down.

We don't always acquire the part we want, or say our parts right. If we keep rehearsing though, while stretching our faith, then life's many plays become clearer.

It's not about how many stars we can place on our stage door, or about commanding more for our performances. If you took the time to read your script you would find that it's about helping someone else with their part. It is giving of one's self from the soul.

Someone is always watching and waiting for you to miss your cues, for the way we deliver our lines has a direct impact on the other players. Do not forget, each play may seem as if it goes on forever. The truth is it only lasts but a moment and in that moment every second counts.

Some of us know this before the curtain opens... some realize it in the middle of the play... some never learn their parts at all... while some never step out from behind the curtain... and for some of us the curtain has closed.

You may order a copy of this parable, printed on a beautiful photo backdrop, by completing the form and following the instructions in the back of the book. To view on-line go to www.glendawalters.com.

Within two weeks of receiving this parable, my supervisor stated that our department was being closed and the company was kind enough to offer me a sales position. At that time I did not feel that selling was my gift. I convinced the CEO to lay me off. He graciously allowed me to work another two months and granted my request. Three years later they closed their doors.

This was not an easy time for me. It meant stepping out in blind faith, making sacrifices until future employment could be obtained.

Weeks turned into months with no feasible employment in sight, so I signed up for unemployment. During this time closets were organized, trips with family members were taken, and there was more time for myself. Upon looking back, I realize that this provided me with a much needed rest. Into the third month, that inner voice reminded me of my promise to volunteer. My answer came by way of an issue of Guideposts, lying on my coffee table. The cover depicted a photo of a Hospice volunteer. I picked it up and read her story, absorbing every detail. After reading the article, I decided to phone our local Hospice chapter.

Upon meeting Linda Hunt, their Community Relations Director, at a local Business Expo I became a Hospice patient volunteer. Into my seventh month of unemployment, a High Point furniture company hired me. I continued to volunteer, and within the year Hospice of Davidson County created a new position, thus hiring me as their Volunteer Coordinator.

For over twenty years I enjoyed a side-line business as well, teaching social and business etiquette, modeling, and pageantry. To this day there are young women I taught, who come up to me and ask if I remember them. It brings me great joy to see the self confidence that these young women carry with them. My past business cards depicted a butterfly, representing new growth. On my first day at Hospice I commented on the butterfly logo, printed on Linda's business card. She replied that she had been instructed to change the artwork to a heart that very day. The butterfly was my confirmation of having been placed there.

After a year of working for Hospice of Davidson County, I began to witness miracles and hear accounts of near-death experiences concerning angels and deceased loved ones. The social workers were aware of my interest in spiritual events, so when they heard of an encounter they would take me out to the patient's home, or share stories with me. Volunteers, along with other acquaintances also told their stories. Two years, prior to my coming to Hospice, that inner voice had nudged me to write about my own supernatural experiences. It was not until coming onboard with Hospice that I began to seriously collect these extraordinary occurrences, along with including some of my own.

I found that by incorporating them into my Hospice speeches, it made for a captivated audience. There were so many requests from groups, colleges, and organizations for these types of stories that I realized it was time to listen to that inner voice, and so this book was born.

PART ONE

BLESSINGS AND ANSWERED PRAYERS

Bring ye all the tithes into the storehouse, that there may be meat in mine house, and prove me now herewith, saith the Lord of hosts, if I will not open you the windows of heaven, and pour out a blessing, that there shall not be room enough to receive it.

...Malachi 3:10

What is prayer, but a form of thought-transmission? By means of it one can draw upon the power of the Divine Mind where all wisdom reposes. Prayer is the line of communication with insights, intuitions, and fresh understandings. With two calm minds working on a problem – God's mind and your mind – you're in.

...*Dr. Norman Vincent Peale*[9]

If we will open our minds to believe, we will begin to witness everyday miracles. Some refer to this as luck, fate, or coincidence. We all have thought of someone we needed to see and have run into him or her within that very week. There were times that we needed something and within days we had that particular item or the information that was needed. My friend Leonard Day (deceased) believed that our guardian angels exchange messages among themselves, thus causing the person or object we need to appear in our lives. I believe that our sincere thoughts and heart-felt prayers bring about God orchestrating our requests. He works through his angels and everyday people to bring about an answer to our prayers and our needs.

If everyone understood the importance of prayer without ceasing, what a difference we could make in the world today. It took me years to understand what this really meant. It is a mindset... leaving an open channel for God to come through. Of course, there is enormous power within heart-felt prayers. There have been many individuals who have come together in prayer for a specific need. Later, they discovered that their prayers were answered. Numerous times, I have asked for confirmations, signs, or asked a question, and the answer, or sign is given to me. Sometimes this happens within the week, often times it takes years, and then there are times it is granted instantly.

This Place That I Go

My parents often took us kids to Cherry Grove in South Carolina on family vacations, and so my love of the ocean carried over to my adulthood. Visions of living by the ocean often played out in my head. My dream was to one day have my very own beach house.

Over seven years ago I walked down to the beach, and while looking out at the incoming waves I silently sent up a prayer that a beach house would come my way. I stated out loud, "one day this will come to pass." It did come to pass less than two years later thanks to my Dad. He bought a second row beach house in Oak Island, North Carolina, and renovated it. It is now in my sister's and my name, with Dad having lifetime rights. While sitting at home one day, reminiscing over past visits to the beach, the following words flowed through my mind:

> In times of unrest I go to this place... this place that I go just for me. There's salt in the air and wind at my back... there's warm sand beneath my feet.
>
> I go to this place to soothe my weary soul, but no one knows this but me. There are cries of seagulls and the crashing of tides... there are dolphins that play in the sea.
>
> As I walk the lone shore, life's reflections pass by, but no one can see them but me. There are sea-shells to be picked and sand dollars to be found... there's driftwood washing up on the beach.
>
> And if I should be missed, would you know where to look... this place that I go by the sea? I think not

you'd find this place in lost time... this place that's known only to me.

For you see, it's well hidden within the archives of my mind... this place that I go just for me.

...Glenda Smith Walters

You may order a copy of this parable, printed on a beautiful photo backdrop, by completing the form and following the instructions in the back of the book. To view on-line go to www.glendawalters.com.

I Am the Deep Blue Ocean

In the warmer months, you will find me at Oak Island, Southport, or Kure Beach, North Carolina. I go there to unwind, visit friends, and to write. While relaxing on the beach one day in March of 2001, the following parable came to me. Luckily, my provisions that day included a pad and pen.

> *Like the Loggerhead turtle that lays her eggs and returns to the ocean, I too must make my way down to the sea. I know not if it's the warm rays of the sun... the golden sand between my toes... or the gentle waves that lap at my feet, but like the Loggerhead I too must make this annual pilgrimage. I find it necessary to perform this ritual with each passing year to restore my soul. Like the incoming tide I'm drawn there to find that inner peace... that glorious solitude.*
>
> *Life has a way of speeding up like a runaway locomotive, sometimes traveling to no specific destination. Many of us try our best to stop at all the stations, but soon find that these stops drain our very souls. Due to the loud roar of the engine we can no longer hear that soft inner voice beckoning for us to*

slow down and listen. We fail to step off the train... to sit down and be silent. It's extremely hard for us to rest... to be quiet, for we have become accustomed to the clamor of the train engine instead of the gentle sounds of the lapping waves.

My footsteps leave imprints in the coarse sand, announcing that someone passed this way. With each crashing wave the ocean gives up its treasure, depositing it at my feet. My steps take me along the shoreline as I stoop to collect a colorful array of spiral and scalloped shells, each one unique and different. This causes me to reflect over my life... my purpose for being here. I find a private swell within a sand dune to spread out my beach towel, hiding me from my everyday obligations. While lying quietly on my back with eyes closed, something incredible happens. I am the deep blue ocean... I become the calming sea.

The only sounds that can be heard are the waves rolling in and the cries of the seagulls circling overhead. The distant rocking of the waves lulls me to sleep. After several hours a lone hermit crab wakes me, dancing across my feet. I stand and stretch, extending my arms out as if a bird in free flight. With eyes closed, I absorb the rays of the tepid sun as it caresses my face. A soothing breeze plays with my tangled hair and then it happens, I am the calming wind...I become the cool ocean breeze.

Too soon my time of solitude ends. I fold up my towel and pack up my things. The car has been loaded, but like many times before I beg my ride to wait for just a few minutes. So I take off my favorite worn sandals, and run to where the incoming water meets the unmoving sand. With eyes closed I stand facing the wind, and then something incredible happens. I am the deep blue ocean...I become the calming sea.

...Glenda Smith Walters

You may order a copy of this parable by completing the form and following the instructions in the back of the book. To view on-line: www.glendawalters.com

All parables come with a beautiful photo backdrop. Shipping and handling is included. A portion of the sales of this parable benefits the Sea Turtle Project in Oak Island, North Carolina.

Months later I returned to the same place on the beach, where these words had come to me. Once again, I spread out my towel and sat down to enjoy the warm rays of the sun. While looking out at the vast ocean, I began to wonder if this parable was meant to be shared, and if so would it cause someone to reflect upon their life. Would the words cause them to ask, “Am I going in the right direction?” After having this thought I looked down to the right of me, and there lay a petrified baby loggerhead. By some means, it had become preserved for all time... attached to a thin reed.

Perhaps this young sea turtle had not been strong enough to make the strenuous journey out to the ocean. The little fellow now rests in peace within a glass box that resides on my dresser. It serves as a reminder that God hears our thoughts and prayers, and answers them in the most unique ways. This small loggerhead keeps me humble, by reminding me that I’m not the writer... for I’m merely the story-teller.

God's E-Mail

I remember the day God sent me an e-mail by ground mail. After four years of being separated from my husband, he began to have numerous medical conditions. During this time I stepped in and took on the responsibility of his care. With the need for sitters, the lost of a job I loved, a new job to learn, my father and husband near death, a pile of medical bills, and having to sell my de-valued dream home, I lost all hope.

The loss of a marriage, selling the home I had entertained our friends in, holding an auction, along with giving away our horses, had placed a large hole in my heart. Our beautiful house, gardens, horses, and over 5 acres of land were what I had signed up for. However, with an ill husband who had never valued being a "team player," those dreams had been dashed. The wonderful world that I had once lived in was no more.

Many sleepless nights were spent worrying about how I was going to meet all the bills that my husband had hidden from me. Oil had sky-rocketed and it was costing several thousand dollars to heat our home each year. My parents and a few friends were there for me, but many of our friends had lives of their own, that kept them too busy to help out. During this stressful time I was thankful for two of my girlfriends, who called each week to uplift me with their positive words.

One day, after leaving an early morning meeting I dropped by Marshalls to exchange an outfit. While sitting on a park bench, waiting for the doors to open I looked down to find two pieces of copier paper at my feet. Upon picking them up I realized that it was a daily devotional, an e-mail meant for me.

The person writing it indicated that it was a message for whom-ever was reading it, straight from the throne room of God.

The message read, that no matter what I was going through, and that even though there were those whom I had counted on had let me down, that God wanted me to know that he would never leave me. I was to know that God was aware of my plight, that he would handle everything in his time, that I must remember that God means for me not to give up.

That was amazing. I so desperately needed to read these words at that very moment in my life. I had often stated to my close friends, that I wished God would call me, so he did what most of us do instead and sent me an e-mail.

It took five challenging years, but I have a stable job now and my life has taken me in a positive direction. My true friends are still in my life, along with new ones. I have a savings account, and I have a side-line business. Although, there are everyday challenges, life continues to be better for my family and me. God always keeps his promises.

A Trip of Renewal

As the scenes played out before me on the big screen, I was unable to resist Scotland's lush countryside. Prior to this movie I had also viewed a movie made in Ireland. Here were two countries, where an American girl could pick up forgotten dreams of her youth. Within weeks, of viewing these two movies, "Maid of Honor,"[10] filmed in Scotland and "P.S. I Love You,"[11] filmed in Ireland I began planning my trip. Due to having had an Irish great-grandmother, I felt destined from the start to make this pilgrimage. It was as if I was meant to visit these two magical places.

As plans began to unfold, family and friends insisted on funding my fairy-tale adventure, even donating frequent flyer miles. After viewing coffee table books of both countries, working with a travel agent, along with studying Frommer's travel guides I booked my trip. Before embarking on my journey I was given a journal with a butterfly engraved on the cover, by my former neighbor Carol. This was another reminder that this trip was one of renewal.

Two weeks before my trip I dreamt of traveling to a grand estate. This mansion had many rooms and gorgeous views. One evening, one of my friends and I were sitting in Barnes and Nobles, looking at large picture books of Ireland. Crystal was turning a page and I caught a glimpse of the very house I had dreamt of. I grabbed the book from her and began reading about the Muckross House. When my itinerary came by e-mail I noted that my tour guide had chosen this very place for me to tour. When I arrived at this place, a sense of familiarity came over me. I'm not sure why I dreamed about this forlorn estate. It overlooks a vast lake, framed by mountains rising up in the distance.

Due to a bad experience, I'm terrified of flying, and to make matters worse, I flew out on 9/11. Eight and a half hours later I arrived at Glasgow's main hub in Scotland. Just like the movies, there at the exit stood a white haired Scot named Ian. He was wearing a navy blue suit and black leprechaun shoes. Ian was holding a white placard bearing my name. Within minutes he had whisked me away to The Jury's Inn in the heart of Glasgow. I felt like someone of importance as he swung the car door open. Ian proceeded to carry my luggage into the inn, while intently going over my itinerary.

Once my suitcases were checked in, Ian took me to Loch Lommond and on to Dunbartan Castle, located high up on a hill overlooking a serene lake. As I looked out across the water a fine mist began to slowly form, rising up from the water. We later stopped at a near-by coffee shop and ordered scones dripping with warm marmalade. As we sat sipping Earl Grey tea out of china teacups we got acquainted. Too soon it was time to return to the hotel. After arriving at the inn we bid farewell and set a time to start out the next morning.

I had read about the famous Horseshoe Bar and the shops prior to my trip, so I sat out that evening for a "walk-about." My first stop brought me to Borders, where I purchased books by UK's very own version of Dr. Phil, known as the famous Paul McKenna. Then it was on to The Horseshoe Bar. As I ventured in, it was like parting the sea. Men stepped aside as I made my way to the back of the room. In my defense let it be known that I would never go to a pub alone, but here I intended to conduct interviews, along with finding affordable meals. Before my trip the American dollar had fallen to half of what a pound and a Euro was worth. The pubs provided a good meal at an affordable price.

At first, I felt as though the word "American Maiden" was stamped across my forward due to the many curious stares, but I soon learned that the women socialized upstairs, while the men discussed their day downstairs over a pint of Guinness. I decided to make the best of it and proceeded to order the country's staple dish of fish and chips at the bar. Within minutes two older Scots introduced themselves. They were interested in talking politics, and like two concerned fathers warned me of staying out too late and not to flash my money about.

On my second day Ian drove me to Edinburgh, where I toured Queen Elizabeth's retired yacht. The Britannica was the yacht that Diana and Charles spent their ill-fated honeymoon. My second stop placed me at Greyfriars Bobby Bar to pay tribute to the terrier, whose devotion to his master brought him world-wide fame. A birdbath with a statue of the little dog, mounted in the center had been erected in his honor. His owner had been an 18th century Bobby. Legend has it that when the bobby died the terrier only left his master's gravesite to beg for food at a near-by pub known as Greyfriars Bar.

Our last two stops were to Edinburgh and Sterling Castle. Here I purchased gifts for my family and friends. After a full day of touring Ian dropped me back off at the inn. Later that evening it was off to the bar known as Babbity Bowster. Once I arrived eight talented musicians started setting up. I was soon discussing politics, this time with two Socialists, one who was not happy with our president. I don't think he even liked the fact that I was an American. However, all the other Scots I ran into went out of their way to make me feel welcome.

The music began to fill the room as everyone began tapping their feet to the lively beat. After a few hours of political talk I slipped out the front door, making my way to a restaurant several blocks up known as "Escape." This was a quaint Italian Bistro, where I learned that locals often met. After listening to the dreams and goals of several waiters of various nationalities, I stepped out to wait for a cab. Standing outside was a young Scotsmen named Michael, who had left his party to smoke a cigarette. It was nice to have someone to converse with as I waited for a ride back to the hotel.

By the third day homesickness had set in, so I decided to have lunch at a near-by upscale restaurant to try to cheer myself up. After finishing my meal I stopped in the restroom to freshen up. As luck would have it I came upon a familiar face, a familiar name. Staring back at me from the bathroom wall was my old friend "Kimberly Clark." Imagine that, this "hometown" dispenser had traveled across the Atlantic to remind me that I was not alone. You see, the Kimberly Clark plant is located in my hometown of Lexington, North Carolina.

On my last day in Glasgow I took the "Hop on and Hop Off" buses, touring historic museums and grand art galleries. At the end of the day I missed my last bus and ran into Michael, who

was standing outside smoking at yet another pub. He invited me inside Burns Bar, where I met his girlfriend Jean and their friends from the BCC television station and The Daily Record News. Here I danced with the Scots and they bought me drinks. In fact, everywhere I went men and women bought me drinks. However, I insisted on drinking very little. It was wonderful to visit two countries who still loved Americans.

After taking photos and jotting down telephone numbers, I made my way back to the Horseshoe Bar, which was close to my hotel. Karaoke was in full swing upstairs, and while standing shoulder to shoulder with local Scots I joined in with a chorus of "You take the high road and I'll take the low road...." Then it was back to my room to pack for my short flight to Ireland the next morning. My trip was a whirlwind of taking in as many sights as possible.

Once again, I took the "Hop on Hop Off" buses and toured such busy places as the National Gallery, while enjoying the solitude of city parks. I toured Dublin Castle with its gold gilded hallways, its display of treasured items, and a tower dating back to 1204. I noted that the Scots and the Irish go to great lengths to preserve a heritage they hold dear. The ornate architecture in both of these countries was well worth the trip alone. If only America could embrace this idea of preserving more of our historical sites.

After two nights in Dublin my itinerary took me out to the West Coast. One of the best ruins to visit would be the Rock of Cashel in Tipperary. It dates back to the 12th and 14th centuries. This is where I made my grand exit, while coming down the steps leading up to St Patrick's statue. A fine rain was falling as our tour guide stated that legend had it... that if a maiden hopped backwards on one foot around this statue nine times she would be married within the year.

The group moved on and I went down, hitting my chin on the last stone step. Thanks to my journal, it somewhat cushioned the embarrassing blow, but later my face looked as though I had been mugged. The Australian couple who came rushing to my aid no doubt thought I had attempted to see if the legend were true.

That afternoon I toured Christ Church Cathedral and went down into the dimly lit catacombs. Rumor has it, that there are bodies buried within the walls. It certainly gave me an eerie

feeling as I followed the winding path around the intricate carved statues. That evening at Quay's Bar a vocalist began singing the popular song known as "Galway Girl," from the movie "P.S. I Love You." This was an omen for me... a confirmation that this trip was meant to be.

Taal, my Irish driver, dropped me off at historical sites such as Trinity College, home to 200,000 ancient books and The Book of Kells. We then traveled to The Burren Region to explore ancient burial sites. The Cliffs of Mohr was a mystical place, rising 700 feet above sea level and going on for seven miles. My driver commented, that we were lucky to have the weather just right, due to the fact that the fog often obscured any view one could have of these majestic cliffs. Birds soared overhead as the waves crashed below. It reminded me of a scene right out of a James Bond, Harrison Ford, or Angelina Jolie movie.

Then it was on to Doolin, known as the music capital of Ireland. Once I was settled in at the Killilagh House I sat out for another "walk-about." After purchasing a Celtic woolen scarf, the shop owner gave me a lift up the steep hill to a castle owned by a South Carolina family from America. I was told that the family's father was heir to a well-known cigarette manufacturer. Sadly, I learned that the owner had died within weeks of my visit. As the sun began to paint a rainbow of colors across the sea, I made my way down the hillside for the four mile trek back to the village. My walk ended at McGann's Pub, where a bowl of steaming Irish stew awaited.

A band of five musicians played and moved their feet to the spirited music. Within minutes an older gent stood up and sang a humorous song about a husband and a wife. While taking in my surroundings I noted the many photos and commemorative plates of Jackie and John F. Kennedy, along with Muhammad Ali hanging on the walls behind the bar. After finishing my meal and conversing with a local farmer I made my way back to the Killilagh House Inn. My room was sparse, but was clean and comfortable. The next morning I found a full breakfast waiting for me in the dining room. I enjoyed conversing with the owners as we enjoyed a spot of tea. We took turns taking photos outside once Taal arrived, and then we were off for my next adventure by the sea.

Tralee and Dingle Bay were two places where the mountains met the ocean, as fishing boats bobbed idly offshore. We slowed

down more than once to allow a herder and his flock of sheep to cross the winding, narrow roads. Slea Head gave one spectacular ocean views, where as Adare was known for its colorful row houses and quaint shops.

Tourists go to shop at the Blarney Woolen Mill, and I was no exception. It did not take me long to come across a pair of dangling, Abalone earrings in one of their large jewelry cases. The place was packed with people from all over the world. Various accents mingled into one as I dined outside at one of the trendy restaurants.

My most memorable stay was at Glin Castle, which overlooks the Shannon River in County Limerick. This Old World country estate has remained in the Fitzgerald family for over 700 years. Generations of painted nobles greeted me as I entered the spacious lobby and a flying staircase beckoned me to step on board. Glin Castle has a vast collection of artwork, fine porcelains, and unique antiques. This majestic home was surrounded by formal gardens, flowing fountains, and regal Yew trees.

Upon arriving, I joined two couples from Greenbay, Wisconsin for cocktails and dinner. After some wonderful conversation and a delicious meal, I retired to my room... a room right out of the pages of a fairytale. My queen size bed sported a Wedgewood Blue canopy, complete with a matching duvet. The "white on white" bathroom had a large jet tub and a shower filled with Crabtree and Evelyn products. I spent the evening lounging in the tub, and later drying off with plush Egyptian white towels. I felt like a princess that night, but felt no green pea between my mattresses. The following morning I showered and dressed, and ran out into the garden to take some photos. My driver showed up too soon and it was time to say my "good-byes." My one regret is that I missed seeing the owner of this grand house by a few days.

For me... these two countries were magical kingdoms filled with talented musicians, an abundance of laughter, painted landscapes, and deep fellowships. I noted that many of the Scots and the Irish I met had less than us Americans, but were far happier due to the kinship they have for one another. Each evening you could hear excited voices drifting across the street from open air cafes, as friends met to share their day. One could not help but get caught up in their shared excitement. Other than a short bout of homesickness, I never felt as though I were alone.

My hired drivers and the hospitality of people from various countries made me feel welcome. It was exhilarating to walk into a restaurant or a pub, and have people come up to me. For some reason people found it interesting that an American would take it upon herself to travel to two foreign countries alone. Of course, it made it easier for me to carry my journal and have people sign it. This journal granted me a certain security, while giving me a reason to record what-ever might be taking place at the time.

Not only did this trip turn out to be one of renewal, but the people I met along the way opened my eyes to how one should view their life. On the final day my driver Taal left me with the following words of wisdom. "We should not dwell on life's challenges, or our past. Instead, we must embrace the lessons learned from the trials that come our way. Family, friends, and even strangers will be sent to walk by our side, so that we never have to make the trip alone, and once we discover this simple lesson then everything else falls into place."

Looking back, on how this journey came about, I'm in awe of how the universe...how our faith truly works. I did not have the money to go on this trip, but once my mind was set, and I believed that it would happen everything fell into place.

A Girl Named Annie

I dedicate the following story to one of my closet friends, Rosemary Russell, who succumbed to appendix cancer this year. Rosemary loved to experience life, trying new products, finding great buys, and traveling to wonderful places. I remember when she attended the Jackie Kennedy Onassis auction in New York. Rosemary and her cousin landed on the front page of a New York newspaper, while showing off their purchases of Jackie Kennedy Onassis' Ming Dynasty, slightly chipped dishes from the Orient. Not only have I lost a close friend, but a traveling companion, and someone to enjoy afternoon tea with. I miss you Rosie.

Annie is a young woman with Down's syndrome who finds untold delight in life's simplest of pleasures. She makes a lasting impression on everyone she meets with her outgoing personality and her positive attitude. I too, was drawn to her at the 1999 Special Olympics World Games. Lynn, her social worker, stated that although Annie had lots of friends she was often sad. You see, she wondered if she had any brothers or sisters. In May of 2001 Annie got her wish when she met the brother and sister she never knew existed.

Going back to June of 1999, Annie and her Arc friends and group leaders attended the Special Olympics World Games. My friend Rosemary and I were there too. Annie was so enchanting that I wrote a story and mailed it to her social worker Lynn. Within weeks, Lynn called to ask permission to place it in Arc's newsletter.

Annie's sister had been searching for years through numerous websites for her sister Annie. When she came across my story on their website she phoned The Arc of Stuebon and identified herself as Annie's sister, and that she lived in Connecticut. She

also informed them that Annie had a brother living in California. Bearing family photos and gifts, Annie's sister and brother arrived in May of 2001 to meet their long lost sister. Below is the revised story that I sent to Lynn.

In May of 1999, my friend Rosemary won two tickets to the Special Olympics World Games. She phoned me to extend an invitation to join her, so on June 26, 1999 we found ourselves at Carter-Finley Stadium in Raleigh, North Carolina. As we took in our picturesque surroundings we noticed that the volunteers were wearing brightly colored T-shirts bearing the slogan, "It's All about Attitude." Rosemary was so impressed with their logo that she purchased a T-shirt for herself.

After downing hotdogs and mounds of ice cream, we learned that our assigned seats were at the very top of the bleachers. They were quite far from the events taking place. We were so disappointed that our high spirits began to wane. Fortunately, our evening was about to change for the better. Within minutes, twenty-some mentally challenged adults and their group leaders descended upon us. They appeared to be in their late twenty's and early thirty's.

While scanning their faces, one young woman with Down's syndrome stood out. This young woman appeared frightened by the height of the bleachers and stood clinging for dear life to her group leader. But once the teams, in their colorful uniforms started parading around the track, she relaxed and took her seat. Her chaperon sat down beside me and introduced herself.

I inquired about the young woman seated on the opposite side of her. Lynn explained that she was Annie's social worker and that Annie and her friends lived in group homes or supervised apartments. She went on to share how Annie had been placed in a home-like setting when she was only five days old. In 1991 she was moved to a family care provider, who became a "grandmother" figure to her. But this loving caregiver soon passed away, leaving Annie alone once again.

She was then moved to an Arc group home. Lynn added, "Annie was chosen to hold the banner in the "Miracle Run" to raise funds for all of the local chapters. She even made the front page of our local paper." Immediately, my heart went out to this "child-like" adult, who had never felt the loving arms of her biological parents.

As I wondered what life must have been like for Annie, Arnold Schwarzenegger emerged on the field and the crowd, along with Annie went wild. A group of Brazilian teens marched out next and Annie started blowing kisses and shouting, "I love you... I love you!" Throughout the evening, with arms outstretched she gave a "thumbs up" to many of the visiting teams as they passed by.

In front of us sat two young people, named Ann and Mike, stealing kisses when they thought no one was watching. Ann had large luminous eyes and long blonde hair, while Mike's cropped cut enhanced his dancing brown eyes. They made an attractive couple, and unless they spoke one would not be able to distinguish between them and any other young couple in love.

Ann took great delight in calling out to the military personnel standing below. As she gained their attention she would giggle and snap their picture. Harold, a tall lanky lad with coke bottle glasses, clicked away for over an hour only to learn that he had not advanced his film. He just shrugged his shoulders while his group leader demonstrated how the vintage camera worked. Once the lesson was learned, he eagerly started to shoot all over again.

After observing this enthusiastic group, it occurred to me that they believed they had no physical or mental limitations. To them, the world held a sense of adventure. They were having the time of their lives. While taking in the scene playing out before us, I contemplated on how I had lost that child-like joy, that innocence somewhere along the way.

Rosemary and I soon forgot about being so far from the field, because Annie and her friends were so entertaining. The fact that they did not have the best of seats made no difference to them. Before leaving, we exchanged addresses with Lynn and promised Annie that we would write. We had hoped to have a poster signed by Arnold sent to her, but I have yet to find a source to do so. What could have been a disappointing evening turned out to be a meaningful lesson through Annie and her friends. Unknowingly, this group had impressed upon Rosemary and me that it is "All about Attitude."

A Prayer Answered

My husband and I started out in my grandparent's small garage apartment. For two years, we saved our money in the hope of building our first home, while we lived there rent-free. The apartment came with a den, kitchen, full bath, and a walk-in closet. We had put up mirrors on one wall of the den to give the illusion of a much larger room. In the eyes of two newly-weds, it was a grand mansion, a playhouse full of dreams.

Whenever guests quizzed us about our bedroom we would smile and point to our walk-in closet. This became our private joke, because the den doubled as a sitting room and bedroom. Our sleeper sofa welcomed friends by day, but put us to sleep by night. My parents, my cousin and his wife had all started out in this same apartment. I felt as though we were following a family tradition.

One of my regrets had been that my great-grandfather passed away within months of our wedding date. The fact that he had not been present at such an important event in my life had left me feeling quite sad. My great-grandparents, affectionately known as "Pop Paw" and "Mama Younts" had lived next door to my grandparents.

My thoughts took me back to a time when my younger brother and I rode home from school in Pop Paw's two-toned, coral and tan '48 Chevrolet. He would pick us up from school two days a week. I can still remember how the strong aroma of a fresh lit cigar filled up the car. My brother and I would immediately roll down our windows once we climbed in. We then proceeded to lean our heads out the windows as far as possible for the short ride home.

Pop Paw would often rest in his favorite lawn chair, smoking his cigar on many a warm afternoon. He would sit under the large oak trees that shaded his yard, along his white picket fence. He loved to sit in his vintage green rocker, watching the cars speed by, many on their way to High Rock Lake. If you ride by their property now you would find it to be the home to Walgreens in Lexington, North Carolina.

I grew up across the street from my great-grandparents home. They lived in a white boarded house with a side and back porch. There was an unattached carport, complete with a shed and a springhouse with a screened in porch. My great-grandfather had built this building for my great grandmother to do all her canning in.

Pop Paw would cross the busy road several days a week to visit our family. You could be sure that he never wore out his welcome. He stayed no more than ten minutes at any given time. Being a man of few words, he was more comfortable sitting alone in his lawn chair, watching the world go by than being among a group of people.

One evening I stood by our open kitchen window, washing dishes and thinking about him. My thoughts went back to my great grandfather having missed my wedding. I was enjoying the cool spring breeze as it soothed my troubled thoughts. Within minutes, an unforgettable aroma floated in on the wind, filling up the tiny apartment. As I stood by the window reminiscing, I found myself enjoying the same cigar scent that I once could not bear to breathe in. I was elated that he cared enough to pay a visit. The familiar scent of his cigar had floated in only to leave within minutes. No doubt, it was his way of leaving his blessing behind.

Once the strong aroma had left the apartment, I ran next door to share my story with my grandmother. After relating my encounter to her, I could not resist making the statement, "You know, Pop Paw never stayed very long whenever he came for a visit."

Kay's Blessing

Kay dealt with cancer the last ten years of her life. She was truly a walking miracle. The disease spread throughout her body, but she continued to work behind the bar at Don Juan's Mexican restaurant in Lexington, NC. She believed that her job provided her a chance to witness to the many patrons that stopped by the bar as they waited for their tables. Everyone who knew Kay loved her, because she always wore a smile and took the time to listen to their problems. She shared with me that she thought her mission in life was listening to, and consoling hurting people. You see, Kay was a bartender, and through her work she heard many sad stories. Time and time again the cancer slowed her down, but she always bounced back. Below you will find a story that Kay shared with me.

"I needed $800.00 for my daughter's tuition, but I could not afford to even borrow the money, so I started praying. I held onto my faith, knowing that somehow the money would be provided. On the day before the deadline, I received a money order for $850.00 in the mail. The name on the money order was unfamiliar to me, but I knew God had encouraged this complete stranger to answer my prayer.

Author's note:

Kay knew to be specific in her request and believed that she would receive what she needed. This way of thinking allows God's universal laws to go into motion. It appears that our thought processes, our faith and belief opens the door to allow our prayers to be answered. This positive way of thinking can place individuals in our path, cause prophetic dreams to manifest, and produce miracles.

Within months of typing up her story, I learned that she was back in the hospital. I dropped by for a visit, only to realize that this time Kay would not be bouncing back. Unfortunately, she was in a coma and there was no chance to have one last conversation. Kay passed away quietly a few days after my visit. She was strong in spirit, and truly an amazing woman. She far outlived her diagnosis, proving once again that our spirits can be far stronger than our bodies.

Be Careful What You Ask For

The old saying, "be careful what you ask for," rang true for me one night when I was in my late twenties. My husband and I often spoke of having children, but we never made that final decision to follow through on that thought. One evening I asked, "What if we were allowed to see what our children would look like, even if we chose not to have any?" Thinking of this statement now, I'm not sure what made me ask such a question.

We soon retired for the evening, but later that night I woke to find three spirits entering my bedroom. Immediately, I sat up leaning on one arm as I watched in disbelief. Like a scene playing out before me, the child actors were lined up by a nun wearing a habit. This caregiver wore her habit low on her brow, and kept her face turned away from me. I sensed that she served as the children's nanny. Each spirit was like a sheer veil that one could see through, and yet you could make out every detail of their clothing and physical features.

The nun spirit lined the young girl up first in front of the armoire; she then placed the younger boy beside the girl. The girl appeared to be between 12-14 years old, and the boy looked to be closer to 6-7 years of age.

While watching the drama unfold, I began to wonder if heaven possibly had a nursery... a place where unborn infants and young deceased spirits were nurtured until they became adults. I later remembered having read books that included accounts of near-death experiences, with individuals seeing guardian spirits caring for babies and children in heaven. They told of viewing young spirits in a type of classroom setting, taught by an adult spirit. Again, we will not know the answers to our curiosity and our questions until we reach the other side.

Turning my attention back to the girl spirit, I noticed that the buttons on her dress ended at her waist. Her shoulder length hair was topped off with bangs. The little boy had a stylish pageboy cut, and he was wearing a dress shirt and shorts. Suddenly, the nun pointed a long finger towards the young girl, and then the boy. I felt that she was indicating that the girl would have come first.

This experience was so unnerving, that I could not remember anything past this point. I later thought of the two miscarriages I had experienced early on, and wondered if these two children were connected in some way. Although, I was not comfortable having this experience, I'm grateful for having my question answered. I now know to be careful what I ask for, because it just might come true.

A Gift from the Heart

Rochella's indisputable gift was her glowing inner beauty. Not only was she beautiful on the outside, but on the inside as well. Once you met her, you had the privilege of viewing the true spirit within. As I grew up, we lost touch with one another until she came back into my life much later. I had learned through a colleague that Rochella had been stricken with Lou Gehrig's disease. During our many visits we would often share angel stories. Through this, the idea was born to start an angel collection for her.

One day while shopping in Oakley's Book Store I came upon the pink porcelain angel that I had often admired when dropping in to pick out a book. I wanted to buy something special, and this angel was a perfect fit. Her flowing robe was a dusty pink and she was sitting up, holding a white dove in her hand. The statue was one that I would have liked to have purchased for myself.

However, the price was more than I had planned to spend at that time and it was before my payday. Sue was throwing Rochella a birthday party and I had been included on the guest list. After much thought, I decided to purchase it anyway. When Rochella opened my gift, her grateful smile was thanks enough.

That afternoon, after her party, my father called requesting that I meet him at my brother's house. I pulled into the driveway and Dad was waiting outside with an envelope in his hand. Once I parked my car and got out, I walked over to where he was standing. He shared how a small investment had made him enough dividends to divide among my brother, sister, and me. My father had not known about my prior purchase. Upon

opening the sealed envelope I found the contents to be ten times more than I had paid for Rochella's angel.

Flowers for Vicky

I was sitting on my front porch daydreaming about all the varieties of flowers that I wanted to plant. I envisioned baskets full of ferns and geraniums bursting with vibrant colors hanging from my porch. The thought of mums and daisies, planted as borders around my house brought a smile to my face. There was only one problem; I did not have the money to buy flowers. I'm retired and live off social security. Flowers were an extravagance on my fixed income.

The following day, my sister Clara called to see if I would ride with her to a local greenhouse. I was not feeling well, but decided to go anyway. Once we arrived we walked among the rows of potted plants and flowers until I became tired and excused myself to wait in the car. Within minutes my sister and a clerk came out carrying four large Boston ferns, four red Geraniums, several large Hibiscus plants, along with Shasta and Gerber daisies. They made several trips, filling up the back of the car.

I assumed that Clara had purchased them for herself. I was disgruntled that she would most likely ask me to help her plant them. Since I did not feel well, I was dreading this task. Once all the plants were loaded in the car my sister slid behind the wheel and began to cry. I asked what was wrong, feeling ashamed of my recent thoughts. She stated that, "No one can ever deny there is a God in heaven." She then shared the clerk's testimony.

I learned that the shop owner had been praying all morning for God to send someone who needed the flowers. She wished to give the flowers as her tithe offering. All she asked in return was that she might receive a blessing on Easter Sunday, which happened to be the next day. When I had entered her shop that day an inner voice spoke to the clerk, stating that I was the one who

should receive her floral offering. Each spring, as the flowers began to bloom, I'm reminded of her gifts...God's gifts to me.

Author's note:

Victoria was my mother-in-law. She shared this story with me many years ago. She was one of the most interesting storytellers that I've ever known. I always admired the array of vibrant colors that grew each spring around her front porch. Sadly, she passed away several years ago from complications due to diabetes.

Mum's the Word

My husband announced one evening that he wanted to have two couples over for dinner. One was a business associate of his, a realtor who worked for a top producing realty company. I knew she sold the higher-end homes, so I wanted everything to go smoothly for my husband that particular evening.

With the grocery list in hand, I headed for the local grocers. Rolling my cart past the rows of flowers, I stopped to admire a crock of cream-colored mums. I remember picking them up only to set them down three times before finally settling on a small bouquet of flowers. Unfortunately, my busy schedule had kept me from running by the bank. There was only enough money in my purse to purchase the necessary ingredients, with only a small amount left over.

On my way home, I could not stop thinking about how those mums would have looked sitting on our front staircase. I arranged the flowers in a vase of water and placed them on my oak sideboard. I could not help but admire their reflection in a nearby mirror. The main dish had just come out of the oven as the guests begin to arrive. The first one through the door was the realtor. She introduced herself, and with a big smile on her face handed me the largest pot of cream-colored mums I had ever seen. The crock was three times larger than the ones at the grocers.

God had read my thoughts and had given me more than the desires of my heart, by way of a lovely lady named Ida Rose Dillon.

Domingo to the Rescue

We once lived in a Williamsburg style home in the country on five acres, and owned three Paso Fino horses. Paso Finos were originally bred in South America for their smooth ride and their outstanding stamina. They have a natural gait that works somewhat like a locomotive in motion. I could stand at my kitchen sink and enjoy watching them run while I washed the dishes.

One evening, while preparing a late dinner my husband came to the back door. He shouted for me to call our next-door neighbors, due to Major having escaped from our barn. Sam related that he had been cleaning Major's stall when he jumped the wheelbarrow and got away from him. I feared the worse, that in the darkness he might be hit by a car or run into barbed wire fencing at neighboring farms.

After calling our neighbors they went out and mounted their horses, while Sam started out on foot. I turned on the outside light and stationed myself in the front yard in case Major decided to head back to the barn. I stood waiting and praying for help to be sent, and then something miraculous took place. The pounding of horse hooves could be heard in the distance, coming up our long graveled drive. Two horses... running neck and neck came into view... throwing gravel up as they left a dusty trail behind them. Major was being led to the barn by a much smaller horse. This familiar looking horse was bay in color with four black stockings.

Both horses were running at full speed, as they rounded our winding driveway on their way to the barn. Racing behind them, I arrived only to find our horse, Major, standing alone in the barn. I quickly put him in his stall and began looking for the

other horse. By this time, the others had returned to the barn to regroup. I related what had happened and they joined me in searching for the other animal. We never found a trace, not even an extra set of hoof prints in the soft dirt.

The answer came to me later that night, why the horse had looked so familiar. Suddenly, I knew that this phantom stallion was Domingo, who had died of colic the prior year. He was smaller in stature, dark bay in color, with four matching black stockings. It was suggested that I must have seen Major's shadow and thought it to be another horse. The horses had been running within the shadow of our house, so this was not possible. I believe that Domingo was sent that night to find and lead our horse back to safety.

An Answer to Prayer

My husband, Toy, worked for the city cutting trees. He also had a side-line tree service business. He was trimming a tree when his safety harness broke, plunging him thirty-four feet to the sidewalk. An eight year old child, who was staying with her grandmother heard his cries. She convinced her grandmother to summon an ambulance, and Toy was taken to a near-by hospital.

After running x-rays and tests, they discovered he had a broken thighbone. His doctor stated that a steel rod would need to be temporarily inserted to support the bone until it mended properly. However, my husband's condition was not stable enough to perform the surgery at this time.

I saw him the following day and was alarmed to see how pale and listless he was. Further X-rays revealed clots in his lungs. His fever began to spike and his condition quickly deteriorated. The ward he was in was so hot, that I phoned his doctor and asked that Toy be moved to a private room.

The next morning a nursing assistant was bathing him as I arrived. I decided to step into the hall until she was finished. Standing in the corridor was our mail carrier, Henry. I told him about Toy's accident and that I was worried that he might not pull through. He told me that each Saturday night the men at Shiloh Methodist Church came together to pray for the needs of others. As he was leaving he stated that he would be sure to add Toy's name to their prayer list.

As I entered my husband's room I noticed that he was having difficulty breathing, so I found the head nurse, who in turn called his doctor. They immediately moved him to ICU and Toy's

nurse promised that she would call if there were changes in his condition.

I was so exhausted that I went home to rest for a few hours. After falling asleep for several hours, I felt as though someone touched me and told me to call the hospital. I immediately phoned my husband's nurse and she stated that there had been no change, so I fell back to sleep until morning. After rising early on Sunday morning, I dressed and picked up my mother-in-law, arriving at the hospital around 10 a.m.

As we walked into Toy's room I noticed that his room appeared to be glowing. This wonderful feeling of peace came over me the minute we stepped into his room. A nurse stood at the head of his bed. She stated, "There's been a big change in Toy since you phoned last. He knows about the accident, that he is in the hospital, and that he has eaten." As the nurse continued to talk to Toy's mother I went to the nurse's station to phone Toy's doctor. He told me that my husband was not out of the woods yet and promised to look in on him that morning. After an evaluation, Toy's doctor felt that he was strong enough to go through with the surgery of repairing his leg.

When I came back into the room I noticed that the room no longer glowed and the nurse had disappeared. It was then that I realized that the nurse had been an angel. On the morning of Toy's surgery a man rushed into his room and asked, "Toy, do you believe in prayer? You better, because there are thirty-four men who prayed for you Saturday night. I'm Rev. Northington from Siloah Methodist Church."

His surgery ended up being a huge success and Toy was able to come home after spending only seven days in the hospital. Within a few days a couple from our Sunday school stopped by and I shared my angel story with them. They became so excited and asked what day and what time this had taken place. I stated that it was around 10 o'clock on the previous Sunday. I learned through this couple, that our Sunday school class had started praying a few minutes before 10 o'clock on that same Sunday morning.

Author's note:

In Toy's case, the strong faith of thirty four men praying earnestly, along with a Sunday school class, produced a miracle. Not only did they listen to the urging of the spirit to pray for this

family, but they prayed while believing that God would intercede for Toy. The answer to our prayers may not come in our time, or play out the way we would like it to. However, it will come about in God's timing. Circumstances happen, and we are devastated by the loss of a job, our health, or the loss of a loved one. But often something good can be taken from each situation to benefit our spiritual growth, or to benefit another person if we are open to it.

Toy lived in good health for many years until he succumbed to Alzheimer's. Although he is no longer with us, his miracle continues to live on in the hearts of those who hear his story.

Miracles Through Faith

"You were told that you would receive it tonight... yours is not a blessing, yours will be a miracle," announced the spirit-filled minister, as he stood before me. On August 18, 1998 my co-worker, Marilyn, extended an invitation to attend a revival at her church on Brown Street in Lexington, North Carolina. The Reverend Shell had invited anyone who needed a blessing to come forward, so I accepted. His words had startled me. What miracle could he be speaking of? The following day I recorded the date and the Reverend's words in my journal.

A week later the answer came. On August 24, 1998 my father had a massive heart attack, while running errands in town. Fortunately, he was able to drive himself to the local hospital. When he arrived at the emergency room my father had someone call me. After I reached our local hospital an attendant directed me back to where a doctor was already working on him.

As my father lay on a gurney wincing in pain, he proceeded to give me instructions on what to do about his vehicle and other matters. I remember asking how he felt and he stated that it was like an elephant sitting on his chest. It was then that the doctor told him to be quiet as he performed a procedure called "The Clot Buster." After this they airlifted him to a hospital that was well known for their heart specialists.

Immediately, fluid began building up within his body. They drained two liters from his lungs as soon as he was somewhat stable. Each day the doctors could give us little hope. On the day they shocked his heart twice, one young doctor stated, "If it is your father's time to go then neither I nor you can do anything about it, but I have seen miracles here, so pray." There was that

word "miracle" again. Little did this young doctor know, but he gave me the confirmation I needed to hear.

And so I prayed, along with my family. Our friends prayed, while encouraging people from all over the world to join in. Churches and Christian television stations placed my father on their prayer chains. A missionary from San Salvador called one of our friends to say that his whole mission was praying for him. It was awesome to know that people around the world, who had never met my father, cared enough to pray for his life.

Day by day we weathered the storm. A wonderful nurse, named Charlene encouraged Dad to fight, as she showered him with encouraging words each week. One doctor told us continuously that if he made it, he would most likely be mentally challenged. They placed my father on a respirator, and for three weeks kept him in a semi-induced coma. Each time they tried to bring him out of it, he fought the respirator.

It was extremely heart-wrenching to watch him struggle each time. Finally, thanks to Charlene, his doctor performed a tracheotomy. This proved to be the turning point of his recovery. The head physician had given us the grim report that much of his heart had been damaged, but after a month, he called the family back in to share that he could not understand how only a third of his heart was damaged.

For someone who had been sheltered all their life, I found myself thrown into my father's world of rental property, building houses, and opening up a Mexican restaurant. I was forced to take a leave of absence from my Hospice position. It was like taking a giant jig saw puzzle and trying to put the pieces in the proper place.

Fortunately, I was not alone, and my friends kept me uplifted. My father's business associates offered advice. Co-workers sent food and paid my hospital parking fees. Cards flooded into the hospital, friends visited, and people phoned every day. My family divided up the many tasks, and helped me all they could.

Looking back, I see the many miracles that took place. For example, an errand had placed Dad near our local hospital when his heart attack began. The first series of tests had revealed that his heart had been severely damaged, but after starting a prayer chain we received the report that his heart did not show as much damage.

During our many visits, we met families in the waiting room who also needed a miracle. These same families prayed for, and encouraged one another. We grieved with those whose family members who did not make it and rejoiced with those who did. Through all the events that took place, I leaned not on my father's diagnosis, but on the evangelist's prophecy and the young doctor's words of faith. Each time I stepped on the elevator to go up to his room, the same scripture would come to mind. "This is the day the Lord hath made, be glad and rejoice in it."

One afternoon I met Shirley by the elevator, who was having a difficult time rolling her IV pole. She expressed that she would like to go down to the outside smoking area. As we conversed in the elevator, I learned that she was having surgery to remove a tumor in her leg the following morning.

Once we reached the outside area she turned to me, and with tears in her eyes said, "I know you do not know me, but would you pray for me?" I had always felt more comfortable praying in private, but as people sat sipping on soft drinks and munching on snacks we bowed our heads and prayed. I've often wondered what happened to Shirley. I hope that if she reads this she will contact me if she can.

I feel blessed to have been a part of a much bigger plan... a plan that involved people who needed our prayers as well. After two and half months, my father was released from the hospital. Another two months had gone by when I received a call from his physical therapist. She stated that she had been trying to reach my Dad for some time. I asked her why, and she replied that she needed to start working with him on his physical recovery. She was stunned when I told her Dad did not need therapy, that he was playing 18 rounds of golf at that very moment.

Once my father recovered, we celebrated at his favorite restaurant, Romano's Macaroni Grille in Winston-Salem, North Carolina. It turned out that our waitress, who also worked at this same hospital, had been Dad's physical therapist. Once she left the bill, Dad stated, "I feel that I've been brought back for a reason, but I do not know why." At that moment I knew only to reply, "Dad, he said; seek and ye shall find."

In 2008, while visiting Ireland, I received a call from a family member that Dad had made it through triple by-pass surgery, but he was not doing well. He had not been feeling good, but had insisted that I go on my trip anyway. The day I flew out my sister

was taking him to his doctor. My family had wanted me to enjoy myself, and had waited until the end of my trip to phone me at Glin Castle. I flew home as soon as I could. This time he was on a respirator for almost two months. Again, there were hundreds of people praying for his life.

On the eve of my Dad being moved the next day to a vent center, I visited him. As he lay hooked up to a respirator, I shared that if his condition did not improve by tomorrow he would be sent to a skilled nursing facility to recoup. I did not wish to use the words "Vent Center," because Dad had recently lost a good friend who had been in one for seven months. I was banking on my father's fear of nursing homes to work for him.

My Dad received yet another miracle by the next morning. His nurse called to say that he had begun to work harder and had shown vast improvement since the day before. Therefore, they did not move him. Within a week he was able to breathe on his own.

Today, Dad can no longer play more than nine holes of golf, vacuum, or change his bed linens without becoming winded. As a family, we pitch in and do what we can to help him. My father's determination and positive attitude keeps him living a somewhat normal life. His wisdom has influenced my life, on how I now view challenging situations and challenging people. He reminds me that through our many losses we grow "in spirit," and that when one door closes God always opens a bigger door.

I thank God for giving my Dad more time, and for preparing me for what was to come. I also wish to thank Reverend Shell for having the courage to pass on God's message that night, and for the doctor who spoke words of faith and hope to me. I now make it a point to call Dad more often, and meet him for lunch or dinner as much as I can. Having worked in a Hospice setting for over thirteen years I realize that our time here can slip away at any given moment. Due to so many Hospice volunteers, family members, and close friends passing away, I've learned to make time to spend with those who mean so much to me. I've learned not to wait to tell others how much they are loved and appreciated.

PART TWO

BETWEEN TWO WORLDS

The last enemy to be destroyed is death.
...I Corinthians 15:26

"I am standing upon the seashore. A ship at my side spreads her white sails to the morning breeze and starts for the blue ocean. She is an object of beauty and strength. I stand and watch her until at length she hangs like a speck of white cloud just where the sea and the sky come to mingle with each other. Then someone at my side says: "There, she is gone!" "Gone where?" Gone from my sight... That is all. She is just as large in mast and hull and spar as she was when she left my side and she is just as able to bear her load of living freight to her destined port. Her diminished size is in me, not in her. And just at the moment when someone at my side says: "There, she is gone!" There are other eyes watching her coming, and other voices ready to take up the glad shout: "Here she comes!" And that is dying."

...Henry Van Dyke[13].

At Hospice of Davidson County, we once distributed a leaflet entitled, "Gone From My Sight" to our Hospice families on our initial assessment visit. This same pamphlet, authored by Barbara Karnes includes the parable above.[14] "Gone From My Sight" prepares and walks one through the stages of dying. It is a guide to prepare families, whose loved ones are terminally ill, on what to expect.

For those of you who have been to an ophthalmologist, you're aware that they have you look through an opthalmometer while certain lenses are switched in and out. During this process the eye doctor is asking you which one is clearer. Well, one to two weeks before one crosses over, it is as if you are looking through

another set of lenses, ones clear enough to include your spiritual surroundings as well.

Individuals who are born with or develop these so-called "clearer lenses," along with a "keener" awareness are known as gifted or clairvoyant. Their spiritual gifts help us to believe that our souls never die.

Much has been written about near-death experiences. Physicians have documented NDE survivors seeing a golden light and angels, traveling through a tunnel, communicating with deceased spirits, along with seeing Heaven and Hell. While working for Hospice, numerous Hospice families and volunteers told of remarkable accounts shared by a loved one who died and came back to share their experiences.

Two of the most remarkable and detailed near-death accounts possibly ever written, is Rebecca Springer's near-death narrative, "Within the Gates," along with Dennis and Nolene Prince's interpretation of Marietta Davis's "Nine Days in Heaven." Ms. Springer tells of traveling "in spirit," to heaven as her body lies dying in a foreign land. She recounts daily activities and reunions with those who had passed away. Her story goes on to describe iridescent pearl walkways lined with gold and overflowing fountains throughout a lush setting. She shares with her readers vivid descriptions of mansions and universities.[15]

"Nine Days in Heaven" is a true story of what 25 year old Marietta Davis experienced in 1848 when she fell into a coma for nine days. During this time she stated that she visited both Heaven and Hell and was shown many of the universes' secrets.[16]

Today's modern science, along with our advanced medical care has made it possible to bring more people back from death's door. Hospice families often stated that a dying family member told of seeing deceased family members, angels, and even Jesus before they crossed over. Not only do these manifestations bring peace to the dying, but they bring closure to those left behind. Death is like traveling to a distant land. Upon arriving, we find the landscape so beautiful and the atmosphere so tranquil, that we wish to stay forever.

Tom's Visit to Heaven

In Carol Zaleski's book, "Otherworld Journey" she points out that as far back as the Middle Ages, some individuals experienced first a hellish experience and then a heavenly one during a NDE.[17] These same experiences continue to take place within NDE's today. The next story is just such an account in Tom's own words:

In October of 1985, my head began pounding due to pressure building up within my brain. My family doctor gave me something to calm my nerves and sent me home to rest. When I started blacking out my doctor sent me to an ophthalmologist who in turn sent me to a neurosurgeon. After looking at my x-rays the neurosurgeon determined that I had a brain tumor, along with blood clots in my legs. He immediately made arrangements for an ambulance to transport me to a hospital in an adjacent town.

Upon checking in, the blood clots that had formed in my legs began moving to my lungs. This caused me to black out due to lack of oxygen. When I woke, there was a young man dressed in a long sleeve tunic gown standing by my bed. He extended his right hand, which I took. I remember glancing back at my body lying on the bed as I stood up, telling myself that this was just a dream.

With his other hand the young man made a sweeping circular motion and a tunnel opened up within a nearby wall. Three dark spirits appeared as we entered the opening, taunting me for several minutes. I later related this to the three strong temptations that had haunted me throughout my life. Once the tunnel filled with golden light they vanished. My companion and I then flew swiftly through this new dimension. It was as if this soft amber

light was drawing us closer. Once we came out of the tunnel I noticed a ravine straight ahead. We took a sharp turn to the right and traveled down into a deep cavern.

This place was built of rock and smelled of sulfur. We came to a sudden stop on a ledge, and the young man instructed me to look through a steamy glass window. To my horror, there was this volcanic lake of fire. Although I could see no one, wails could be heard from spirits crying out for help. Looking to my right I noticed a door without a handle. My guide touched the door and stated, "Those that go through this door never come out."

Once I sensed the heat radiating from the misted glass and door, I turned to my guide and said, "You must be an angel and this must be Hell, so why am I here?" The angel turned to me saying, "You had to see this place before you could go on to the next." The angel extended his hand once again and together we left the cave. We then walked in mid-air across the deep ravine that I had viewed earlier.

As we reached the other side I felt love and peace encompass me. There was a beautiful meadow that seemed to go on for miles. Instead of a sun in the sky, there was a natural golden light that illuminated everything. The temperature was very comfortable, as if it were 70 degrees. It was if this light intensified every cell in my body. I knew the answer to every question about God and the universe. All I had to do was ask, and the answer would be given telepathically. I suddenly felt loved and forgiven at the same time.

As I continued to make my way through the meadow, a large oak tree came into view with a stream flowing beside it. When I reached out to touch the tree, the angel blocked my arm, declaring, "Do not touch this tree." The thought came to me that if I touched it I could not go back. In the distance, I could see a large city sitting on a hillside with three gates made of an iridescent material that resembled mother of pearl. I told the angel that I wanted to go to the city, and he replied, "When you arrive at the gates, do not enter in, for you will not wish to leave."

Once I thought of visiting this place again, I was instantly transported to the middle gate. As a sports car enthusiast, I remember laughing to myself and commenting, "Let's see a Ferrari do that!" Running my hand over the smooth finish of the middle gate, I noted the transparent opaque pearl finish. The walls were massive and had twelve layers of gemstones.

Suddenly, hundreds of people started coming up to greet me. A female spirit walked up to the gate and I sensed that this spirit would have been my sister. We enjoyed conversing for a few minutes and at the time, I made a mental note to share this with my mother. Later I learned from my mother that she had a miscarriage in 1947.

As hard as it is to believe, standing before me were all these biblical characters. The first to speak was the Apostle Paul. He said, "Tom, you and I have something in common. Before coming here my eyesight was beginning to leave me too." I saw eleven of the disciples, along with Moses, Noah, and King Solomon. My experience seemed to go on for years, but it only lasted twenty minutes.

Instantly, I'm in the throne room, surrounded by this bright light. I saw a golden chair with intricate carvings depicting angels. There were angels the size of cherubs flying in and out of the room. Within this light... this vaporous cloud... God spoke to me about the purpose of my life. He went on to share why I had to go through so many health issues. I was told that I would only retain a portion of the information that was given to me... so that it would not hinder me in my mission on earth.

In an instant, I woke up in my hospital bed with a sheet over my head and a toe tag. A nurse was busy removing my IV when I pulled the sheet off my head. She ran out, screaming for a doctor to come immediately. Instead of one, seven doctors showed up within a matter of minutes with oxygen. One doctor removed my toe tag, while another doctor tore up my death certificate. They were baffled how I had been clinically dead for twenty minutes without showing signs of brain damage. I kept asking them if I was having a heart attack and they finally told me to be quite.

They ran a series of tests and x-rays, but the tests did not explain what had happened. Within days, I learned that they planned to schedule surgery to remove my brain tumor. My doctor stressed that due to the location of this tumor, that it would be a delicate surgery. He went on to say that there was a possibility that I might die or wake up paralyzed. His words brought back fearful memories of waking up as a child, and not being able to move for several minutes.

The surgery was rescheduled eight times due to my numerous infections. On the morning of my eighth scheduled surgery, I got down on my knees and pleaded with God to heal me. I finally

was able to say, "Your will... not mine... be done." Once these words were said a gust of wind came into the room, rustling the sheets on my bed. A voice said, "Tom, do not be afraid." I stood up, turned around and fell back on the bed. Standing before me was Jesus in a flowing white robe at the foot of my bed.

Jesus then said, "Tom, you will live through the surgery, but when you first wake up you will be paralyzed on one side. Do not worry for within two weeks I will restore your ability to walk. You will encounter infections and complications. As these things manifest themselves, remember to rebuke them in my name out loud. All this is being done to honor and bring glory to My Father in heaven." He then disappeared before my very eyes, and I fell into a deep sleep. I woke up when they were prepping me for surgery.

Nine hours later I woke only to realize that the prophecy foretold was beginning to unfold. After the doctors tested my nerve impulses they told my parents that I would never walk again. I told them they were wrong. I shared my experience with everyone. The physicians became so concerned that they sent a psychiatrist to evaluate me. The psychiatrist tried to persuade me that the surgery had caused me to hallucinate. I shared with her that I took psychology in college and knew the difference between reality and a hallucination. After I stated once again that I would walk in two weeks, she threw up her hands and left my room.

Like my doctors, my male physical therapist did not believe me either. In fact, he stated that he did not care to hear my story... that he considered himself an atheist. He told me that the only movement I would have would come from my right side only. He stated, "You'll never walk." I could not help laughing at his unbelief. For two weeks, I continued to pull myself up to the parallel bars. All I could do was stand up and sit down, while supporting myself with my arms.

On the fourteenth day, I struggled to hold onto the bars. My therapist took this opportunity to mock me by stating, "Today is the day that you said you would walk, but God must be asleep." I felt up to his challenge and sent up a silent prayer. Within my mind, I heard the words; "Don't say anything, let's show him." I began to feel an electrical current surging through my entire body. Suddenly, everyone's attention was on me. With the help of the bars I was able to walk.

Needless to say, the physical therapist was speechless. My doctor was from Czechoslovakia and was also a self-proclaimed atheist. He agreed with my other doctors, repeating over and over... "It's impossible." Immediately, this doctor hooked me up to an EMG meter. He was baffled, because my nerve impulses were not registering. He went as far as hooking up a paraplegic sitting close-by. The machine registered the same for him. He ran more tests, made me do all sorts of exercises, but could find no physical reason to support the fact that I was able to walk.

On the day that I was released, this same doctor from another country took it upon himself to wheel me out to my car. As we reached the vehicle he leaned over and whispered; "Tom, you almost make me believe there is a God." I learned later that he had returned to his homeland to practice medicine. I would like to think that my miracle gave him a newfound faith, and that he now shares his faith with others.

Author's note:

Tom and I met in a Sunday School class. It took great courage for him to share his experience with me. It's rare that one feels comfortable enough to talk about a hellish experience, much less sharing that they saw and spoke with biblical characters. Most of us fear that if we share such an experience, that our friends and families will not believe us... that people will make fun of us. I even hesitated myself in including the part where he meets biblical characters. He was so adamant that he saw these famous men of the bible that I felt it necessary to not leave this important detail out.

Some individuals fear that by stating they saw Hell, their peers will judge them harshly. If more people would come forward and share such experiences, it would help put to rest the myth that only angels and heaven exists. It might also stop the ongoing statement; "We worship such an awesome, loving God that he would never send anyone to a place called Hell...that Hell only dwells within a mindset that we create for ourselves." God is a loving spirit, but even he has set-up his own ground rules.

Fear of any kind binds us and prevents us from taking a leap of faith... a positive step forward. If we overcome that fear, there is always that one person that our experience gives hope to. It could possibly turn someone's life around.

Tom had shared that the three dark spirits represented the three temptations that he had fought most of his life. Like Tom, we are human, and we will be tempted and challenged throughout our lives by the dark side. However, we can pray a hedge... a white light... or mirrors around us every day to act as our protective shield. We can bind and rebuke the dark side. We can do the same with our mindsets that have been handed down to us by our forefathers, our parents. We can do this by saying out loud each day, I bind... rebuke... and cast off the spirits of control, depression, anger, or whatever you may be fighting against. This is a way of protecting and ridding ourselves of strong negative traits and dark spirits.

You've heard about "the sins of the father being handed down." Well, most of us are aware of alcoholism, mental illness, or suicide running within a generation... a family. But many are not aware that there are negative, harmful emotions that can be handed down too. It is up to us, working with God, to break these chains... these patterns started by our forefathers. I once knew this vivacious woman who had many friends. She had risen to the top of her profession. Sadly, and at a young age, she took her life by the same means former family members had chosen.

We had planned to have lunch the following week. I searched for answers by way of her friends, to learn what would have caused her to commit such an act. I learned it was due to a pattern that had been formed long ago... a family mindset... a curse that she allowed to be handed down to her. Therefore she accepted what she thought to be her fate and ended her life like other family members who had done so before her. Unfortunately, we are rarely taught how to protect ourselves spiritually... how to denounce certain spirits or traits that bind us... how to be aware of and how to prepare for spiritual warfare.

The Night I Died

My former father-in-law (Dwayne) was one of my closest friends. After he passed away I began to have visitations and dreams, in which he would tell me how certain scenarios would play out. One night I dreamt that I got up, went into my Mom's kitchen, and there was Dwayne sitting at the kitchen table waiting for me.

In my dream I made a pot of coffee and then poured a cup for each of us. We sat at the table, conversing like old times. After several minutes, my father-in-law became serious and told me that I needed to get my life in order. I cannot recall anything after he made this last statement. However, the next morning I found two empty coffee cups sitting on my Mom's kitchen table. During this time I was going through a turbulent time, having lost my job and my fiancé'.

My father-in-law's most recent visit took place during a near-death experience. I was attending an out-of-town conference, and had ordered a diet coke at a near-by restaurant when I began to feel nauseated. After stepping outside I frantically hailed a cab. Once inside the vehicle, my nausea increased and so did the pressure in my chest, so I asked the cab driver to take me to the hospital. Thanks to my former wife, who is a nurse, I knew my symptoms indicated that I was going into cardiac arrest.

The minute the cab pulled up to the emergency room I was whisked away to ER. I began to black out numerous times as they used the paddles to shock my heart. I later learned that my heart had stopped beating four times. Once the medical staff began working on me, the ceiling lights began to spin before my eyes and suddenly I was transported to another place... another realm. There sat my former father-in-law with his feet propped

up on his well-worn office desk. With a concerned stare, he peered over his glasses and asked, "What the heck are you doing here? Why are you not at work?" I stated, "I'm here to make a payment on my account."

In life my father-in-law had owned an appliance store, and I had made monthly payments on items I had purchased from him. "Your account has been paid in full. How's your Mom now that your Dad has passed away?" asked Dwayne. I assured him that she was doing well, but was now in a nursing home. "You can head on back to work now," Dwayne stated, abruptly ending our conversation.

The scene then switched to a blinding white light, illuminating a large white cross. It was so bright that it hurt my eyes. I remember asking where was this place that I had been brought to, calling out to anyone who might answer me. Only silence replied.

Then I turned around and caught a glimpse of my Dad walking up a path within a beautiful landscape. He was with someone I did not recognize. "Hey Dad," I called out as he smiled and waved. He never slowed down as he continued walking, conversing with his friend.

The scenery changed a third time and I found myself in the middle of my grandmother's garden. She was hoeing around her vegetables. "What are you doing here?", she asked. I told her that I came to help her with the garden. "I appreciate it, but I've already picked the ripe vegetables for today. Give your mother my best and now you go on back home. We will have plenty of time to talk later," said my grandmother.

It was then that I woke up in my stark hospital room, connected to IV's and machines. Once a stint was in place my condition stabilized. Later, my doctor suggested that I write down my experiences in a journal. Through all these different experiences I was aware that a presence was with me. I could feel the pressure on my back as if someone was nudging me along the way.

I've often wondered why God saved me. Until I find the answer I know only to live each day as if it were my last. And with each day I will continue to try to do acts of kindness along the way.

Going Home

My sister Leta was never her "happy go lucky" self once her husband passed away. She missed him terribly and often talked about him as she recanted their happy times together. After turning eighty-six my sister's health started to fail her, and she began to speak of going home. On one of our visits my sister shared that she often prayed that God would send her deceased husband to escort her over when it was her time.

Several times a week I would stop by to check on her. On this particular day I washed her hair, and after placing her under the dryer I stepped into the kitchen to make a fresh pot of coffee. When the last drop of liquid flowed into the carafe I stepped around the corner to ask Leta if she would like a cup herself.

There sat my sister under the hair-dryer, but she was not alone. Standing behind her, with his hands resting gently on her shoulders was my deceased brother-in-law. As I looked on, a smile crossed my sister's face as she slumped over. Not only was I happy that God allowed me to see my brother-in-law, but that he had granted my sister's final request as well.

The Dark Force

After caring for my brother-in-law, who passed away with cancer I decided to become a Hospice patient volunteer. The Volunteer Coordinator found a perfect match for me within my own neighborhood. After sitting with my patient and running errands for over a year I quickly became a part of their family. Once my patient died I began to look for another way to give back, so I enrolled in a nursing program.

Upon receiving my diploma I found a position at a local hospital. While working as a nurse I had a terrifying experience with a dark spirit. One day one of our patients was within minutes of passing away. As I entered his room I spoke to his wife, who was sitting by his bedside. I suddenly felt compelled to lay my hands on him, and pray for his safe passage to the other side.

As my hands touched his right arm, a dark spirit came out of his body and threw me up against a near-by wall. The force of the blow literally knocked the wind out of me. In fact, I was so weak I could only crawl out of the room. Once on the other side of the door I continued to pray for his soul as he lay dying.

After this patient passed away his wife confided in me that she too had seen the dark entity come out of her husband. I only wish that I could have done more for him.

Author's note:

In life and in death it appears that God allows us to make our own choices. We can choose to do good deeds or do evil acts. We can give into our addictions or we can ask for deliverance of them. We can be passive, crave acceptance and follow the crowd, or we can stand up for what we believe in. It is my belief that in death, we can choose to walk into the light, or refuse to enter

in. Just like the choices this man made for himself, (both intentional and unintentional), we can choose to allow the dark side to slip into our lives, by the choices we make.

Clay Finds a Way

On the first day, I matched Floyd with a patient, whom I will refer to as Clay. He immediately began to share a fascinating story with Floyd and myself. Below is the account Clay gave us that day in his own words:

"I farmed until the cancer got the best of me. I've been having these visions at night. Several nights a week an angel appears and escorts me up to the gates of heaven. The ceiling opens up like a matinee, revealing the wonders of another world. It is so beautiful there that I want to stay, but I'm always told that I'm not ready to step over.

But on this last visit Jesus appeared and asked me why I did not stay. I told him I could not find a way to release myself from down here. I've already said my "good-bys" and given my possessions away to my family and close friends. I've been so weak for so long that I'm ready to go." Having said this Clay became silent and indicated that he was tired.

After Floyd and I left we discussed what we had just heard. Floyd was truly amazed, for this was the first time someone had shared a near-death experience (NDE) with him. This match provided Clay with a new friend, along with giving his wife a chance to work in her garden. On this first visit Clay and Floyd found they had a common interest in farming. Unfortunately, their friendship was short-lived due to Clay's fast-growing cancer. He shared this account with Floyd and me just three weeks before his death. This was an eye-opening lesson for both of us. He was relating the struggle that goes on between our spirits trying to cross over, only to be held back by our minds, our bodies, and our concerns for others.

I will always be grateful to Clay for having the courage to share his experience with us. His story helped Floyd to deal with his own serious health issues before he too passed away. Within three weeks of matching them, Clay finally found a way to let go of this world and step into the next one.

Eternal Flames

Minnie was a resident in a skilled nursing facility that I was once employed by. As her nursing assistant I often brought up my faith. However, after several conversations she professed to be a staunch atheist and instructed me not to speak on the subject again. One day Minnie was screaming out my name, so I ran into her room to find her in pain. Her nurse was making a futile attempt to console her, while holding her down as she thrashed around in her bed. Through tears she cried out, "Betty, put out the flames on my feet, they're coming up on my legs!"

For the next two hours, until she died I tried to console her. She was so overwrought that I could not have a rational conversation with her. It appeared that not only was Minnie physically feeling the heat, but she was seeing the flames as well. It is my belief that Minnie was on her way to the place we know as Hell.

Author's note:

I've interviewed numerous certified nursing assistants and nurses from various nursing homes, hospices, and hospitals. Each stated that there was a distinct difference in the dying experience for someone who dies believing in God, as opposed to those who died without. These medical professionals stated that not only do their patient's exhibit a look of fear, but also act as if they are experiencing some unseen torment.

As I stated earlier, some would have you believe that only Heaven exists, that our all forgiving God would never create such a place called Hell. However, according to some who have experienced death and returned, Hell is a real place where souls still have their senses, feelings, and their memories. According to some I interviewed, who were given a glimpse of Hell, it is a

place that once a soul enters in, there is no way out. Like Tom's angel stated, in "Tom's Visit to Heaven," "Those that go through this door never come out."

Agnes and God's Grace

At seventy-eight my mother knew her time was near. The cancer began to spread throughout her body and her pain increased. Soon we had no choice, but to check her into a local hospital.

While she was in the hospital Mother shared how one day she was reflecting on whether her actions had made a difference in the lives of others. As she became wrapped up in her thoughts, she suddenly found herself in a glorious meadow surrounded by bright yellow flowers. She told of how the lush green grass swayed to the rhythm of a gentle breeze. In the distance she could hear a choir of heavenly voices singing, so she decided to walk toward the sound of their voices. She continued to feel the same stirring breeze around her.

My mother came upon an enormous wall, layered in different hues of brilliant stones. A large angel stood guard at the massive gates. Looking past him, she saw dazzling sunbeams bursting forth from within the walls. As her eyes focused on the angel, she noticed that his wings were large enough to encase his entire body. "What is your name?" he asked. "Agnes Tucker," Mom responded. "You cannot enter in just yet," the angel said. "I wanted to see who is singing," my mother replied. The angel pointed to another path that she was to follow.

Leaving the green meadows behind, Mother began to notice as she continued walking on the other path, dead and decaying debris everywhere. Instead of beautiful trees and vibrant flowers, there lay blackened stubble. Rounding a bend in the road, she saw a blazing lake of fire with people bobbing up and down, screaming for mercy. Terrified, she quickly turned to go back and almost ran into Jesus standing before her.

"You must make a decision, and it has to be now," he exclaimed. My mother fell to the ground and hid her face. She stated, "I'm so sorry for the sin in my life, I choose you. I thought I belonged to you." "Many have a form of godliness that leads them down the road to destruction," said Jesus. Again, my mother apologized as Jesus leaned down to take her hand, pulling her to her feet. He looked deep into her eyes and said, "You must go back for a short while, for you have much to do, but your time is short." Instantly, my mother found herself back in her hospital bed. She decided to keep her visit to the other side to herself.

Several days later, she was moved to my brother's house. During my mother's stay she related that four angels were standing guard, one in each corner of her bedroom. She shared that as they fluttered their wings, she could still feel the same gentle breeze she had experienced in heaven. For three days, my mother pondered what the message had meant. The third night her meditation paid off, for Jesus told her in a dream that she was to share her near-death experience with others.

As soon as she woke the next morning, she told everyone about her glimpse of Heaven and Hell. Our family began to wonder what had happened to Mother. Her face was radiant, as she shared her story over and over again. Within four weeks, she was back in the hospital. While there she continued to share her testimony with anyone who would listen. Her doctors and nurses were amazed at her enthusiasm as she lay dying. Late one afternoon, Mother stated, "Our separation will be short."

My mother managed to make it through yet another day as I sat at her bedside. On this same day, around 7:00 a.m., she speaks of seeing Jesus standing at the foot of her bed. By 9:30 a.m. she sits straight up in the bed and exclaims, "My earthly work is now done and he's taking me home today. Call the family in because I'm going home." Everyone had gathered around Mom when she announced that her deceased parents, husband, brother, and grandparents were in the room with her. "There is my welcoming party! And look, a feast has been prepared for me. The table is set and it is so full. I can't wait, because I am so hungry." Several family members misunderstood and tried to feed her, but she refused to eat.

By five p.m. she raised her head and said, "He's still at the foot of my bed. Can you see him? Is it time yet? Just a little longer?" She nodded and rests once again. By 9:00 p.m. she

asked everyone to go home, stating, "You won't let me go home. If everyone will leave, then I can go home." All but my youngest brother decided to leave. By 8:00 a.m. the next morning he realized that Mother was lingering because of him, so he gave her permission to go on. He later told the family that after he spoke these words, it was as though she quietly drifted off to sleep.

Author's note:

At Hospice, we have observed patients who go into a comatose state, often wake up a few days before death and appear to be quite alert. Through the observations of our Hospice medical staff, it appears that we are often granted a time of closure... a time to say our good-bys. Many families mistake this as the miracle they have been praying for.

Often family members encourage the dying to eat when they do not wish to. The body has a way of shutting down, preparing itself for death. Near the end you no longer have the urge to eat. This is a natural process as the body prepares to release the spirit.

Unfortunately, many family members fear death, staying away when the end is near. This can be a time of closure and forgiveness. Through my work in Hospice I've found that the dying experience often reunites estranged family members. This is a time to make amends... to heal old wounds.

Beth expressed that she was glad she had not missed her mother's last moments. She went on to say that her family had experienced the beauty and peace that death could bring.

The Fateful Skiing Accident

At the age of twenty one I had an out-of-body experience that made a profound difference in my life. My friends and I were water-skiing, when two large speedboats came by. The boats caused the water to become turbulent and I fell, swallowing too much water. Within seconds, I began to drown.

After several futile attempts to surface, my mind gave into my fate. It was then that I relaxed and experienced no discomfort. Scenes of my childhood flashed through my mind. It was like watching a video that had been fast-forwarded. I saw myself at two years old, making mud pies under a large plum tree. Then my life review picked up speed and stopped when it reached my twenties.

At this precise moment, I found myself standing before the most awesome, loving being. This wonderful, perfect peace filled up every cell within my body. My senses told me that this glowing spirit was Jesus, and I could feel his unconditional love and acceptance for me. Words cannot express how great it felt to be standing in front of such a powerful being.

Then I heard these words, "You must go back, for your work is not yet finished." I remember thinking that I did not want to go back. There was this loud thud, and instantly I was back in my body. It was at that moment I heard my husband and friends exclaim, "She made it... she's breathing!" They had pulled me from the water unconscious and held my head over the side of the boat, forcing water out of my lungs. From that day forward, I knew that only one thing truly matters, and that is the love and acceptance we have for one another.

Author's note:

Faye mentioned that once she stopped struggling and accepted her fate she was no longer afraid. I too have felt what she is sharing. When I was around eight years of age my Dad and I were walking out into the ocean, when a large wave knocked me off my feet. Due to the strong current my Dad and I drifted apart. I'm not sure he was even aware that a wave had knocked me down.

Little did we know that the current had formed a rip tide as we walked out into the water. The strong pull of the ocean would not allow me to surface. At first, my fear was overwhelming, but I soon gave into the fact that my life was ending. Flashes of my childhood played out in my mind. It was like watching a movie fast-forwarded. I was standing with my new bike... I was playing with my hula-hoop. Several more images came to mind as I floated face down in the turbulent waves. Then I could feel someone's hands reaching down and pulling me out. To this day my father states that he was not the one who saved me. He had not been aware in those few minutes... that I was in trouble.

Faye donates numerous hours helping others through her work at Hospice and Palliative Care Center of Alamance-Caswell County. She spends much of her time presiding over The Hospice League in Burlington, North Carolina. She is in charge of putting on their annual Flea Market each year. Faye and her three hundred-some volunteers take in, organize, clean, and repair thousands of items. They store them in donated tractor trailers throughout the year until the event is held. Faye is able to have everything donated, right down to the power.

When we first met, she was riding around on a golf cart within a huge warehouse, megaphone in hand, lovingly giving orders to her dedicated volunteers. She was once again setting up the Big Hospice Flea. After introductions were made I asked her how she ended up volunteering for Hospice.

She told of how she was blessed with not having to work, so she wanted to give back by volunteering. Faye shared with me of how she had moved there from Florida, and having been active in volunteering for an organization there, she wanted to continue to do so. The story goes, that she choose to volunteer for a local soup kitchen, and set-up an appointment with their Volunteer Coordinator. It was winter, so she donned her fur coat and drove to the local Mission House.

While knocking for some time at the back door, a local vagrant walked by, and called out; "Lady, they stopped serving at two o'clock." She laughed as she told her story, stating that she took this as an omen and departed. The next day she called the local Hospice chapter and has been volunteering there ever since. Faye and her volunteers raise over $300,000 each year for their "In Patient" Hospice House. Hospice and Palliative Care Center of Alamance-Caswell County is blessed to have such a driving force of volunteers, along with Faye's passion behind them.

A Look of Horror

While working for a local nursing home, there was one patient that was difficult to handle. The staff did not look forward to having him as a resident. Paul was ninety-nine years old and was bed-ridden. He came to us with an ill disposition and would often throw his bedpans at the CNA's. There was never a kind word for anyone. Instead, he preferred to scream obscenities at anyone who entered his room.

Due to a stroke, his roommate could not speak coherently. He could often be found crying out in the middle of the night as if he could see some dark unseen force. The nursing assistants, including myself questioned why he behaved in such a manner.

As Paul lay dying under my watch one night, this look of terror came over his face as he stared at the bottom of his bed. There was this fear in his eyes and the temperature in the room became extremely cold. I distinctly remember watching this cylinder... this fine mist come out of his chest. It was then that the white mist was met by a dark spirit standing by his bed. I was so terrified that I ran out of his room to find a nurse. From that night forward, we noticed that Paul's roommate slept peacefully.

Sandra Turns Back

I became extremely ill after battling a hacking cough and cold for two weeks. By the time my husband convinced me to go to my family doctor I was too weak to stand up by myself. The doctor informed me that my cold had turned into walking pneumonia. He made arrangements for me to be admitted into the hospital the next morning. Once we arrived home, my husband put me to bed and he went into the den to watch T.V.

After going to bed I began to feel rather faint and found myself drifting off. While lying in bed my spirit left my body, went behind the bed, traveled through the wall, up through the ceiling and down into the hall. I then turned around and traveled back into my bedroom.

While viewing my lifeless body lying on the bed, I became aware of a presence standing beside me. While turning my head to the right I saw this radiant angel. He communicated telepathically, that it was time to go. After he had repeated his message, I began thinking of my children growing up without me. I was worried that they would have a disadvantage in life growing up with only one parent. Suddenly, I felt myself being pulled back into my body.

A Father Reaches Out

I lay for weeks in a hospital bed fighting for my life. I had contracted a fatal kidney infection, leaving me weak from the lack of potassium in my body. My weight dropped drastically to only sixty pounds. A tube was placed into one of my veins, so that large doses of potassium could be pumped throughout my body. Within minutes, I felt a strange sensation and shared this with the nurse before drifting off. I learned later that the nurse had checked my blood pressure and had notified my doctor that I had no pulse. I had an allergic reaction to the potassium.

Doctors and nurses ran into my room and began to frantically start another IV with a different solution. My spirit floated over the doctor and nurses, as they tried to resuscitate me. I could not understand why everyone was so concerned about the lifeless body that lay on the bed below. After all, I felt perfectly fine. Then I saw my husband enter the room, and watched as his face completely drained of color. Suddenly, the room took on another dimension. It was one of beauty and serenity with a stream flowing by in front of me.

As I viewed this beautiful place, my father appeared on the other side of the stream. He reached his hand out to help me cross over, and my first impulse was to pull back. I had always feared my father. In my younger years my Dad had a violent temper, along with the fact that he could not be trusted. Before his death he had tried to change his controlling ways, but I could not forget the nightmares he had caused me throughout my childhood. The minute I rejected my father's welcoming gesture, I was back in my body again.

Author's note:

After our interview, Tricia shared that she was confused why her Dad had been the first one to greet her from the other side. Perhaps her father was reaching out for forgiveness.

Memories of My Great Grandmother

Before breaking her hip twice and becoming bedridden, my great grandmother loved tending her flowerbeds. She grew a variety of roses and zinnias', sweet williams, hydrangeas, along with other plants and herbs. Her love for gardening transferred to my brother and me. When planning my own gardens I chose the same color of Sweet Williams and Hydrangeas that she grew. I can still see her wearing a colorful sunbonnet, leaning over one of her rose bushes, taking in its fragrant perfume.

Her home was built beside my grandmother's house. It was located near the railroad tracks, and her flowerbeds surrounded all four sides of the house. When she was much younger, she could be found serving many a meal on her back steps to the hobos that stole rides on the trains that came through. She had very little, but she shared what she had, and never turned anyone away.

Her hip never mended properly, so she was forced to spend agonizing days, bedbound until her death. While sitting up in bed one day, she began having conversations with deceased family members and friends. She would even look in the direction of the person she was having a conversation with, while addressing them by name. Of course, no one in the family could see anyone in her bedroom. After all, these visitors were for her eyes only.

She told my grandmother during this time that she had visited heaven. While there, she stated that she had walked with Jesus in a beautiful garden and had seen a lovely little bird

that had kept her company. Three days later my great-grandmother, whom we affectionately called "Maw," returned... no doubt... to tend her gardens in heaven.

Judy's Last Words

A Hospice nurse recants:

At thirty-nine Judy learned that she had gastric cancer. This form of cancer is usually very painful, but through morphine we were able to make her comfortable, while managing her care. There was something that stood out about Judy. She seemed to glow and always had such a positive attitude. It was evident to anyone who visited with her, Judy was not afraid to die. She was looking forward to crossing over.

One day she requested that I come over as she called her family members into her room one at a time. She announced to all that she was going to see heaven before them. When the time came she called everyone into her bedroom and exclaimed; "There are so many silver angels and the light is so bright. Jesus, if you're ready for me I'm ready to go, if not let me rest." With these last words Judy raised her arms, and with her face beaming she gave up her spirit.

A Mother's Love

Betty, a former CNA recants:

My grandmother and I were talking one day and she shared with me a remarkable story. One evening when my grandmother was much younger, she and her children decided to retire early. Back then many of the rural people had no heat in their homes. In order to stay warm in the winter months my grandparents kept an ongoing fire in the den and their bedrooms when they were home. My grandfather worked third shift and was not expected home until the early morning hours. After tucking her children in she stoked the fire in each of their bedrooms.

Once the children were safe in their beds, she too bedded down for the night. She found herself falling asleep as soon as her head hit the pillow. After several hours she woke up to a cold room. Upon waking she noticed that the flames in the fireplace had died down. Suddenly, she noticed the sound of soft music playing off in the distance. She recognized the melody. It was a lullaby that her Mom often sang to her at bedtime. Then unseen hands began to pull her covers up to her chin and tuck her in. My grandmother shared that she was so frightened she could not move for hours. Finally, my grandmother ventured out from under the covers. She shared with me that once the music stopped playing, the fire in the fireplace had sprung back to life.

When my grandfather arrived home the next morning, he carried with him a telegram. My grandparents did not own a phone. Residents received news in this small remote community by way of telegrams. When she opened up the paper that my grandfather held in his hand, it was a message from a close relative stating that her mother had died the night before.

Author's note:

Betty's great grandmother, upon leaving this earth had tucked her child in one last time. This loving gesture was her way of saying good-by. When a deceased loved one pays us a visit they might choose a familiar scent or song, move a familiar object, or give a telepathic message to be identified by. Betty's great-grandmother knew that her child would be able to recognize the familiar lullaby.

A Prophesy Fulfilled

Tim and I had been married for fifteen years when he had his first heart attack. I was at home when Tim called, stating that he did not feel well and was on his way to the house. After reaching home, he managed to walk in the back door and into the den before he collapsed.

Just the day before my son and I had been at the mall where firefighters were giving out large red stickers to place on home phones with the local EMS phone number. This was before we had "911" as an option. Fortunately, my son had placed them on all of our phones. After dialing the EMS number, I began performing CPR and the ambulance arrived within seven minutes.

While Tim was in the hospital, he had an out-of-body experience. He stated that as he soared over the church we attended, God told him that he would grant him five years to raise the funds for a new church complex. He also made it clear that once this project was finished, he would be called up to heaven. A local news station got wind of my husband's story and interviewed him.

For five years, we lived a wonderful life. I worked in sales for a large manufacturer, while Tim stayed home due to his health issues. He devoted the time he had left to raising funds for a new softball field and recreation center for our church. The funds were raised and the complex built. Five years later my husband suffered yet another heart attack, but this one proved to be fatal. I found him lying in the garden. I immediately started CPR, but could not revive him. Although, I knew what had been prophesied, I could not stop thinking that maybe I could have done more.

After my husband's death, his cardiologist told of having an uncanny experience that he could not explain. He stated that he was standing on a street corner in Greensboro. When he looked across the street there stood Tim on the opposite corner. He shared that he was stunned, as he watched my deceased husband throw up his hand, shouting; "Thank you for all you did for me." He went on to say that once my deceased husband had called out to him, he simply vanished before his very eyes.

Annie's Angel

In October of '94, my ninety-one year old mother lay dying of cancer in a nursing facility. One night Mother and I sat up all night talking about the good times that we had shared as a family. She suddenly turned her head towards the window and her eyes lit up. "Linda, can you see the angel?," she asked. Mother described how beautiful she was and that her wings were trimmed in gold. She went on to say that her angel had come to take her home. She stated that I could not go with her, because it was not my time. Throughout the evening, Mother lay in silence... looking towards the window... stating that she wanted me to use angels in some way to benefit Hospice.

At that time, I worked for Hospice of Davidson County as their Director of Community Relations. My mother continued to make the same statement, but I could not understand what she was trying to tell me. As the evening wore on, she became very excited, as` she told of another room... another dimension opening up before her... and that she saw an open door. I encouraged her to go towards it and within minutes she passed away peacefully.

That week I dreamed of white angels adorning a large Christmas tree. The idea came to me to do this in memory of our Hospice patients, while honoring other individuals. I went to work, acquiring donated supplies, and entrusted a host of volunteers with the job of making angels from white lace. With a $5.00 donation, a white angel would be placed on the tree "In Honor Of" or "In Memory Of" a loved one. In turn, they could choose a handmade Victorian ornament or angel to take home. By way of the dream, I was able to fulfill my mother's final wish.

Author's note:

Thousands of lace angels have been made over the years... angels that have brought back wonderful memories and closure to those left behind. This was how our local Hospice Angel Tree project was born. Each year local banks and businesses graciously allowed us to set up trees in their lobbies. The local churches and volunteers pitched in to make angels and ornaments. There were over 300 individuals involved. The project was such a success that many local newspapers interviewed Linda. Four Hospices from other counties sent representatives to take pictures and ask questions.

As individuals came by to purchase an ornament, many shared with us their heartbreaking stories. Some talked about their battle with sickness, while others told of the loss of a family member. Seeing an angel, placed with their loved one's name on it, brought a contented smile to many who were grieving. People came by to view the trees that were set up in numerous locations. Circles, clubs and other organizations dropped by to give donations to Linda's project.

One man stood looking sadly at one of our trees, as Linda manned the table. He told of his son's recent death in a motorcycle accident. He shared how he could have been a better father, that his son had died never knowing how much he loved him. "Do you think if I place this angel on the tree in his memory, that somehow he will know that I do love him?" asked the grieving father. Her answer had been "Yes."

I believe that this man's son can feel his father's love. I think those who were close to us and crossed over know when we are happy or sad... and they can feel our love for them. After all, our love and our personalities are all we can take with us to the other side. This was one of many questions asked and stories told. Over the years that this project took place, these trees have helped countless people heal their grief. Linda no longer works for Hospice, but she continues to touch the lives of countless others in a hospital setting.

A Final Peace

I can only recall meeting my grandfather three times. My mother was a young girl when her father walked out of her life. She called him Jim, because he was never a father figure to her. Ironically, he looked like Jackie Gleason; and like the role Jackie played in The Honeymooners, my grandfather was a city bus driver. Unfortunately, he also had a drinking problem.

Mother had two brothers and one older sister. Her sister died at the age of eighteen from an asthmatic attack. The pressures of supporting a large family on a bus driver's salary proved to be too much for my grandfather. He met and later married a younger woman that rode on his bus route each day. They were married before he told her of his prior family.

My grandmother's salary, at the local textile mill did not begin to cover their expenses. This forced my mother and her sister to work after school and during holidays at the local soda shop. Mother even fibbed about her age in order to be hired. My mother's grandmother lived next door and her two spinster aunts and an uncle lived across the street. Had it not been for these giving and caring relatives my mother and her family might have become homeless. This same uncle would often pretend to find coins on the ground. When my mother and her siblings came for a visit he would give them the coins that suddenly appeared on the ground.

My grandfather only saw his children a few times each year. His absence from my mother's life was very difficult for her to understand as a child. In his late fifty's he stopped drinking, but ten years later he learned he was terminally ill. Upon learning of his diagnosis, he invited his children and grandchildren over to his home to choose from his collection of glass vases and dishes.

I chose an amber pedestal candy dish and a small Japanese vase. It was at this time my grandfather spoke of dividing items up between my mother and her brothers. That was the last time I saw my grandfather. I've always thought that his gesture of giving away his vase collection... was his way of asking for forgiveness.

Weeks later he became so sick that his wife checked him into a local hospital. As my mother stood by his bedside and my father stood by the door, my grandfather expressed that he wanted to go home to "The big house." Then he began speaking with someone, who neither his wife nor my parents could see. My mother asked him whom he was talking to. He replied, "I see a bright light... Roby, my brother is there in the light... he's waiting for me by the gate... he's calling my name... I must go now." Roby had been my grandfather's youngest brother.

With those final words my grandfather joined his brother on the other side. He had finally found the peace that he had yearned for. In the end, my mother was able to forgive her father. She understood that his addiction had been so great that he had done the best he could under the circumstances.

David's Race with Time

At the age of thirteen I was given a tetanus shot just two hours before my next sailboat race. I decided to walk to a friend's house for a visit before the race. As I started up the hill and then down towards my friend's house I suddenly turned around and returned home. My actions puzzled me.

Once inside my house, I went over to the refrigerator to take out a gallon of ice cream. While holding the carton I suddenly sensed that something was terribly wrong, because I was no longer breathing. I ran into the den where my father and sister sat reading. Looking up from her book, my sister screamed out that something was wrong with me. By the time my father reached me, I had turned blue and passed out. My father picked me up and ran to the car. He raced to the hospital, as I lay in the front seat unconscious.

While my father sped down the street, I found myself hovering over the top of the car. Through the roof I could see my body lying on the passenger seat beside my dad. I also saw that my father was highly distressed. This concerned me so much that I tried in vain to communicate with my dad. I wanted him to know that everything was fine.

When he pulled up to the emergency room doors, my mother ran out to meet us. She worked as a physical therapist there and had received a call earlier from my sister, who told her of my condition. When I saw my mother's worried expression, my spirit went back into my body. The pain in my chest intensified as I regained consciousness. I remember taking in a gulp of air. I learned later that the tetanus shot had caused anaphylaxis shock, which causes the lungs to collapse. Needless to say, I never had to take another tetanus shot.

Author's note:

I met David while working for the Furniture Market in High Point, NC. One day our conversation led to talking about spiritual experiences, and this was the story he had shared with me.

Anita's Mother

On July 13, 1994, my mother had an appointment to see her family doctor about her latest test results. She had been experiencing excruciating pain, and her skin had become jaundiced. I was with her when the doctor gave her the devastating news, that she had pancreatic cancer. He advised her to see an oncologist immediately and speak with her minister. I will always remember the fear I read in her eyes that day.

After meeting with the oncologist, mother chose to go through with the surgery he had recommended. It made her more comfortable, but they found evidence that the cancer was in an advanced stage. The oncologist gave her six months to live. Mother lived out her final months, as if she were not ill at all. "If I have to die, I have to die. I do not wish to be in pain though," she would say to her children. She never asked, "Why me?" By the end of February of '95 mother had become bedridden, and Hospice was called in.

One Saturday night, mother's color returned to her face, and she appeared to have a burst of energy. Before I go further, I would like to stress that she was not taking any hallucinogenic drug. Suddenly she leaped from the bed, got down on her knees, and demanded that everyone pray. She told us that she was seeing visions of hell. I was extremely concerned, since my mother had always led a Christian life. Sadly, she had lived in hell while on earth in an unhappy marriage. It's possible my mother had to acknowledge and bind that part of her life in order to release herself from her earthly bondage.

"Its torment... its torment... please pray... all of you... hard," she cried out. We all dropped to our knees beside her bed to pray for her protection. My mother went on to say that she could see

things in the room that we could not see. She first saw entities from the dark side, than she saw a radiant light, and a ship waiting to take her home. My mother was also seeing her own mother by her bedside. She mentioned angels floating above her and asked where Paul, her guardian angel was.

Each time Mom prayed, she felt more at peace. After our family had prayed for the fourth time, my mother gave us a thumbs up and said she was no longer in pain. Suddenly she screamed, "Get out of here. Don't let them take me!" I asked to whom she was referring to. She told of two men waiting for her to go with them. She then became concerned that there were far too many spirits in her room.

As I remarked earlier, my parent's marriage had not been a happy one. Mother believed that the stress she endured throughout her marriage had brought on her fatal illness. My father had to pick her up from the floor several times, because she would lie down to rest, and then wanted to kneel again on her bedroom floor. During one of these episodes, she hugged and kissed him. After this show of affection, my father broke down and cried. He had always been very controlling, never allowing my mother to work or have any friends. She did manage to have one secret friend, though.

Mother soon became quiet as she silently moved her lips, speaking to an unseen entity. She later told me that she had been talking with a man standing at the foot of her bed. She mentioned seeing lovely leaves and beautiful violets. The next day she asked to see her minister once more.

When mother decided to let go, she hugged everyone and asked that her hair and make-up be done. She wanted to see the dress that a neighbor had brought by for her, and she chose jewelry to match. We were amazed that she was calmly coordinating her burial attire. Again mother went down on her knees beside her bed to pray. Our family, including the minister, laughed and cried that night as we talked and prayed together. We found this to be a beautiful experience that brought our family closer together.

On a Friday morning, she told us that tonight would be her last night with us. My mother's favorite winter past time had been to sit by the patio doors with a bag of popcorn, and watch it snow. I was now surprised to see large snowflakes coming down outside her window. Her pain had returned and we rushed her

by ambulance to the hospital. As the ambulance took her away I knew that she had been granted her last wish... to watch it snow one last time.

When I arrived at her bedside, the last words she whispered were, "I can't talk anymore, and you need not talk either." After receiving her medication, she fell into a deep sleep. We left when my father arrived the next morning. At 1:15 a.m. the following morning, my mother passed away.

During Mother's funeral, her friend shared with us that she had heard my mother calling out to her. After hearing her voice she approached our minister, and asked to accept Christ into her life. Through my mother's last days, and even in death, she had reached out and touched so many lives. She taught my family through her actions, how to forgive and to love one another, no matter what took place in the past.

Author's note:

I've had the privilege to interview numerous individuals who came back from the dead. Several individuals shared that the dark side tormented them before they proceeded into the light. This is not to say that all who believe in God... in Christ will have this same experience. These testimonies were an eye-opening experience for me, because each of these loving individuals had come from a strong Christian faith. This is why I encourage people to pray that God will protect the dying as they travel into the light.

A Glimpse of Eternal Light

At the early age of twenty-six I developed high blood pressure. While preparing to take a bath one night, I blacked out and fell backwards into the shower stall. After coming to, I discovered that I was in the strong arms of an angel, carrying me swiftly through a dark tunnel. I was no longer in my body, because I felt lighter.

I caught glimpses of gray clouds as we ascended higher and higher through this black void. The blackness soon turned into such a bright light that it illuminated a beautiful landscape. I could feel God's presence, and the sense of love surrounding me. Nearing the end of the tunnel, a voice warned me to go back. Instantly, I found myself lying on the cold shower floor.

Author's note:

Often individuals, who had an NDE shared that an angel accompanied them, as they traveled at record speeds through a tunnel. On January 14,1997 the Winston-Salem Journal carried a story of astronomers discovering the existence of black holes in our universe. The article went on to relate that Albert Einstein tried to prove long ago, that there were massive black holes in the heavens. These vast holes come in different shapes and sizes. They range from the size of an atom to a half-billion times more mammoth than the sun. The larger ones are known as "stellar," and the massive ones are called "supermassive."

The article states that fourteen out of fifteen galaxies have these immense holes. It goes on to say that these holes are normally formed from collapsed massive stars, and any matter that comes near these funnels are taken in by a powerful gravity pull. The story also indicates that a black hole cannot be seen, but

the effects it creates, on near-by stars and gas clouds are highly visible. Scientists believe that these funnels were created at the beginning of time.[18]

In Mary K. Baxter's book, "A Divine Revelation of Hell," she speaks of seeing black holes in the atmosphere. She shares with her readers that in March of 1976, while praying, Jesus Christ appeared to her stating, "My child, I will take you into Hell by my Spirit, and I will show you many things which I want the world to know. I will appear to you many times; I will take your spirit out of your body and will actually take you into hell. I want you to write a book and tell of the visions and of all the things I reveal to you."[19.]

Mary Anne goes on to recant that one night "in spirit" she traveled with Jesus so high into the sky she could see the earth below. Protruding out of the earth and scattered about in many places were funnels spinning around to a center point and then turning back again. She states that they moved high above the earth and looked like giant, dirty slinkys that moved continuously. She insisted that they were coming up from all over the earth. "What are these?" she asked the Lord as they came near to one. "These are the gateways to hell. We will go into hell through one of them," he had stated.[19]

Many people would find it hard to believe that Mary's experience was anymore than a horrible nightmare. And before anyone writes or e-mails me, I wish to make it clear that I'm not endorsing her controversial book. I merely found the scenario, between The Winston-Salem Journal's article and the description that Mary gave of these funnels in the sky as being very similar to one another. Could it be that there are "tunnels" or "black holes" in our atmosphere, going in two different directions, one towards Heaven and another towards Hell? Many people speak of traveling upward at a great rate of velocity when they have a near-death experience. Then there are other accounts that mention another dimension opening up. Of course, we will not have the answers to many of our questions until we die.

A Paramedic's Account

While holding the position of Davidson County's Hospice Volunteer Coordinator, I had the opportunity, along with two of our volunteers, to attend an informative regional workshop in Charlotte, North Carolina. On the last night of the conference, they treated us to a five-course meal, which was followed with a dynamic guest speaker. We were seated around a large round table near the front of the room. After we sat down I turned to the gentleman to my right and introduced myself. I'll refer to him as Doug, who was a paramedic. I could not resist asking him if he had witnessed any unusual experiences while he worked on those who were close to death. The following story was told to me by Doug that evening.

"We were called out to a home where a man in his early sixty's was having a massive heart attack. After strapping him onto a stretcher, we placed him in the back of the ambulance. While in route to the local hospital, my partner and I continued to perform CPR on this gentleman. We observed that his vital readings showed no visible signs of life. His blood pressure had dropped extremely low and he was starting to turn blue, but we continued to do what we were trained to do."

"I had the paddles on his chest for a second time, when the man opened his eyes and grabbed my arm. He looked into my eyes and shouted; "Leave me alone," and then he closed his eyes and passed away for the second time. His words shocked me so much, that I laid my paddles down, and told the other medic that we had done all we could do for him."

Author's note:

Doug had risked his job by honoring this man's last wishes. He respectfully granted this dying man his last request.

Below you will find an article that I wrote years ago. At the time, I was not aware that these words would be for me to read years later. I stumbled across it in a forgotten file at a time when I needed it the most.

Letting Go

Life is an ever evolving process of "letting go" of people, places, things, and even time. It is necessary for us to learn this in order to master our emotions... to grow more "in spirit." After wasted time and numerous disappointments, this heart-wrenching process prepares us for the ultimate test, this art of "letting go."

With each new challenge we are given a choice. We can choose to hold onto sad memories, staying right where we are, even allowing bitterness to creep in, or we can "let go" by not looking back as we bravely trudge forward. If we allow our maker to walk with us and work through us... with the passing of time we will begin to understand that we must "let go" in order to move forward... in order to complete what we are here to do.

Often we must "let go" of familiar places we called "home"... of a treasured trinket we once held... and alas we must "let go" of those to whom we have given a piece of our heart... those with whom we have shared our lives. We must grow stronger emotionally in order to accept the outcomes we cannot change. I'm speaking of the ones we were not meant to hold on to... those things... those individuals we were not meant to keep. In time, through this ever changing process we will discover why we are here through helping others. We gain wisdom through reading books that bring us self knowledge, along with taking time to fellowship with one another.

At times this "loss of self" brings about a brokenness called "grief." There are many steps to work through. First comes denial, we do not wish to believe

what others tell us. Then comes a sense of false hope, so we barter with God. We believe that we have the power to change the outcome, and then comes frustration and even anger, because we cannot change what has been set into motion.

We soon find that we cannot change that other person to fit our needs, or bring back that individual due to a break-up or a death. We must come to know... to respect and acknowledge that each individual is on their own spiritual journey... a different path than our own.

As the clock counts time, there is the loss of youth, health and faded memories. Throughout our life we have chosen our paths, paths that lead us in many directions. There are paths of enchantment that entertain and distract us... paths that keeps us far too busy to enjoy time for ourselves... and even paths that keep us standing right where we are. Then there are roads that lead us to a greater knowledge... a greater understanding.

In time, many of us come to know this... that we must look for that hidden path... that path that leads us to the divine. There are times our paths cross with those of others... paths that lead us to a higher learning of self. If we acknowledge our lessons... if we somewhat conquer our human emotions. and our shortcomings... then at the end of this journey we gain acceptance, as we come together for all time.

Near the end, "sorrow" comes knocking at our door. Then with "time" we invite "acceptance" to come and sit by our bedside, so that we can say our final "good byes." We then travel with our companion known as "knowledge," knowing we will see that person... our friends... our family members once more on the other side.

Remember the movie "Ghost?" At the close of the movie Patrick Swayze (Sam) turns to Demi Moore (Molly), and as he walks into the light his face takes on this urethral glow. He pauses and turns back to look at Demi (Molly), stating; "It's beautiful Molly; you take the love with you when you go."[20]. The love he

speaks of... this unconditional love we have for one another... this all encompassing "knowing"... this is what we take with us when we leave this place.

What better gifts for us to take on our next journey. That path that leads us to heaven...a path where we will discover that we never really lost our loved ones, for they will be waiting for us on the other side to welcome us home. As for the loss of familiar places and treasured things, there are new places to visit, and new treasures to discover on the other side.

PART THREE

MINISTERING SPIRITS

"Those on the other side know what you are going through, and at times cross over to lift you up in spirit."

...Anonymous

"Are these not all ministering spirits, sent forth to minister for them who shall be heirs of salvation."

...Hebrews 1:14

Through interviews with many of our Hospice family members, I was told they had experienced at-least one visitation from their deceased loved one after they had crossed over. Some visited in a dream, while others chose to come in spirit. Accounts show that those from the other side can sometimes break through the barrier between this world and the next. Their messages bring closure and peaceful assurance to those who have been left behind.

For different reasons some spirits choose not to cross over. This could be unfinished business, not being able to let go of places, things, or out of fear of going to the other place.

A Request Granted

My mother and Rochella took turns car-pooling during my early days of elementary school. Each Wednesday afternoon Rochella treated her daughter and me to an ice cream cone at the Lexington Drug Store. Once we moved across town our parents lost touch with one another.

Thirty years later, Rochella came back into my life, by way of her illness. We renewed our friendship as I watched her bravely battle amyotrophic lateral sclerosis, better known as Lou Gehrig's disease. At the time Rochella came back into my life, she shared that she had endured this devastating disease for over eighteen years.

With our many visits, I could have written another book entitled; "Tuesdays with Rochella." We would sit in her den that overlooked her patio and she would often encourage me to finish this book. I remember one day she stated that she felt led to encourage me to use a handheld recorder for all my interviews. I'm sorry to say that I should have listened, for it would have made it so much easier for me during the numerous interviews I conducted.

She knew that I needed a laptop computer, so she prayed about it. Within weeks one was donated to our local Hospice office, with a request that it be given to me to use. It was the exact brand I had been praying for... a Compaq. One of Rochella's friends had passed away, and it had been his. His wife expressed that she was not computer savvy, and thought that I could make better use of it. That was a popular brand when I began documenting these accounts. Needless to say, I was elated.

Rochella was known throughout town as a great "prayer warrior." In fact, it was a known fact that she prayed for many people

throughout town. Her pastor Ray Howell decided one week to hold an evening Bible study on the Book of Revelation. He was wary of what kind of response the topic would receive, so he asked Rochella to pray about it. After over two hundred people signed up for his class, he told her husband to tell Rochella to slow down with her prayers.

People from all walks of life requested that she pray for them. Visitors came to the Baker's home with the idea of cheering them up, but it was the Bakers that prayed for and lifted their guests up. Matter of fact, Rochella had so many visitors that her husband told everyone not to bother ringing the bell, but to come on in. Her Sunday school class named their class in her honor.

Rochella's strong faith touched not only her friends, but strangers as well. In 1994 she appeared on the cover of Carolina Country Magazine with her good friend Sue Wikstrom by her side. Due to the article she became a local celebrity. Strangers would stop her and Ted on the street, and in stores to chat. She never complained as her body slowly succumbed to the disease. Until she drew her last breath, she continued to intercede for others.

On our last visit, Rochella was sitting up in the middle of her bed... becoming frustrated as she tried hard to find a way to communicate. My Hospice experience told me that she had about three days before she would pass on. Due to her weak throat muscles, she had lost the ability to speak coherently. In order to help her relax I indicated that "in spirit" I understood what she was trying to share with me. This seemed to appease her for the moment, and she began to relax.

Before walking out of her bedroom I made a last request, stating, "If you can, please stop by and visit me one last time." She smiled and nodded as I left, with both of us knowing that it would be the last time I would be dropping by.

To some... what I'm about to say concerning my friend will be too hard to believe, but it truly happened. On the evening of Rochella's funeral, after arriving home I retired early. Upon falling into a deep sleep I suddenly woke up, sensing a strong radiating presence standing in the doorway of my bedroom. I'm sad to say that this startled me and I could not find the courage to open my eyes.

Within minutes the entity moved swiftly to my bedside. It was at this moment I knew that Rochella had honored my final

request. As a last farewell, she reached down and gently touched my arm, and then she was gone.

Her husband Ted and daughter Wendy have now crossed over also. It's my belief that they are once again together.

My Grandfather Stays Behind

After my grandfather passed away, my father made arrangements for a sitter to stay with my grandmother each night. Our family pitched in, by rotating each Tuesday to give the sitter a break. A single cot was placed in her living room for us to sleep on.

Within days of my grandfather's passing, my grandmother mentioned to my dad that someone was coming in the middle of the night to check on her. With my grandmother's health beginning to decline, my grandfather had taken over the grocery shopping and running errands over the last few years. He took care of her every need.

It was my turn to sleep over, and we sat up until ten o'clock that evening, telling stories about my grandfather. Her eyes twinkled as she shared his routine with me. According to her he watched the eleven o'clock news, took his bath, tucked her in, and then retired by one o'clock.

After I put on my pajamas she stated that the cot was not comfortable and insisted that I sleep in my granddad's twin bed. With a nightlight as bright as daylight, an old metal clock that ticked loud enough to wake the dead, along with grandmother's heavy snoring I questioned how I could fall asleep that night.

Finally, I drifted off for a few hours until I became aware of another entity sliding into the bed with me. I can only compare it to feeling a type of pressure against me. The body was longer than mine and as it rolled over I felt an arm coming around me. It was at this moment the entity jumped off the left side of the bed, while I jumped to the right. Within my head I heard my grandfather murmur a few words, but could only make out the

words, "bounced off." This led me to believe that he was confused about what, or who was in his bed.

I wanted to know the exact time, so I walked around my grandmother's bed to read the clock on her nightstand. It read one thirty a.m. My mind raced back to hours before, when my grandmother had shared with me my grandfather's nightly ritual. I contemplated on what to do, because faint noises could now be heard coming from the den. I chose to go back to bed.

While relating this story to a close friend she asked, "Surely, you did not go back to that bed and fall asleep?" I replied that there was no reason for me to be frightened of my grandfather in life or death, that he obviously knew that someone was occupying his bed that evening. At that time, I had no doubt that he was sticking around to look after my grandmother.

I have since had another visit from him. Six years ago I decided to move into my grandparent's quaint cottage on a near-by lake. I threw myself into cleaning up and decorating their cabin, along with finding unique options for storage space. With my grandfather's passing, and grandmother at that time in a nursing home, I wanted to display some of their treasured things.

My grandmother loved collecting antiques and miniature figurines that she referred to as "tricks." On the other hand, my grandfather collected tools and fishing tackle, along with making keepsakes out of wood and metal. I thought by having their treasures around me, that it would be as though they were still with me. My grandmother loved beautiful things, and she saved everything. Her motto was if you threw it away today, you will surely need it tomorrow, or within the year. I found that to be quite true, but who wants all that clutter.

When we cleaned out her home we found Jackie O. style dresses, pillbox hats, and pointed high heels that were back in style. There were unique teapots, dishes, and glassware, among numerous other items. By this time my grandmother had succumbed to dementia.

Although, the cottage was quite small it had one of the best views on the lake, along with a outdoor open shelter. I spent many a summer evening sitting on my grandparents' glider... under the shelter, gazing out across the lake. Late in the evening I would often stand on the sun porch, watching a Blue Heron forge for his meal by the weathered pier. Each night the security

light stood watch by the boat ramp. It would cast its light of hope across the waters, giving the Heron an added advantage.

As a family, we were often invited in the summer months to dine outdoors under the shelter with my grandparents. I can still smell the cheeseburgers that my grandfather liked to grill, along with hearing the churn of the ice-cream maker turning out a fresh batch of peach ice-cream.

My grandfather could fix or build almost anything. He worked for his father-in-law, repairing sewing machines in the family's denim overall plant. As you know, mechanical devises often come with an abundance of oil to keep them running. My grandfather was always tinkering with sewing machines or lawnmowers, so he cleaned his hands by washing with lye soap.

On the other hand, my memory of my grandmother comes with the sweet pungent smell of cakes and pies. After living for several months in their cabin, my grandfather showed up in my room at 4 o'clock one morning. His presence that morning came with the fresh scent of lye soap. I had recently gone through some challenging times. Looking back, I feel that my grandfather's visit came out of his concern for me.

Author's note:

We tend to identify the remembrance of loved ones by certain smells. You may think of lilac perfume or the smell of a vibrant rose when remembering a dear friend or your beloved mother. It is my belief that this is the easiest way that they can communicate with us from the other side when they drop in for a visit.

Jerry's Spirit

My brother-in-law was only 48 years of age when he died of cancer. Jerry was like a brother to me. We could talk about anything. He loved to fish and won many professional bass tournaments. Jerry was also an avid deer hunter, a sport that his son Jeremy has carried on. He loved the outdoors and both activities so much that it was rare for him to join in on special family occasions. Once Jerry's brothers learned of his illness they took it upon themselves to take him out once a week for dinner.

After he passed, he made numerous visits to those he loved. Sam and I had only been home for two hours from attending Jerry's funeral when Jerry made his first visit.

My husband Sam was watching television in our den and I was busy emptying the dishwasher. As I turned away from the kitchen sink I became aware of Jerry standing across from me within a corner of the room. Although, I could not see him, there was no doubt in my mind that he was truly there.

Throughout my life I could see far more with my feelings... my senses than my physical eyes. This sixth sense has given me an edge... sometimes a warning when accepting a new position, or when meeting another individual for the first time. This was the same gift I was using as Jerry's spirit made it known to me. I told him that we loved him and would miss him, going as far as to say, that when he crossed over, he would still have the opportunity to enjoy nature. Due to the disadvantage of not knowing what he was thinking or saying, I was soon at a loss for words. It was then that I turned back to the sink, telling him good-by in this life.

Within the week Jerry stopped by again one afternoon as Sam was napping on the sofa. I was sitting up, on top of our bed covers reading. Our bed provided a direct view, down the hall and into our den. However, my view did not include my husband sleeping on our sectional sofa. Our home included a vaulted ceiling with a skylight in the middle of the room.

While looking down the hall something caught my eye, so much so that I slowly closed the book I held. Floating down from the ceiling was a ball of light, the size of an average size melon. It glimmered like silver fish scales dancing across the water at sunset. In stunned fascination I watched the ball float towards the place that I knew my husband was sitting.

There were two reasons I chose not to walk into the den. First, my husband can be the best of skeptics, and second I had this strong feeling not to intrude. I knew from experience that our deceased loved ones sometimes communicate through dreams. For many of us, it is the only time that we are silent... it is often the only way they can get a message through to us.

Later that same evening, Sam shared that he had had a dream about his brother. He dreamt that he walked into the den and there stood his brother Jerry. He then stated that in the dream he called out to me stating, "Glenda, you'll never guess who's here. It's Jerry." In Sam's dream he had asked his brother how could it be that he was in the den with him when he had passed away days ago. It was then that Jerry had smiled at him and slowly disappeared. Sam went on to add that his teeth were so brilliantly white. Jerry had a habit of chewing tobacco, which had somewhat discolored his teeth. Sam's reference to his teeth made me think of the experience I speak of concerning my grandfather after he passed. He too had the most vivid white teeth in my dream.

Before Sam's mother died, she shared that she saw a ball of light as she sat by a near-by mirror within her home. She stated that when she saw the ball of light in the mirror behind her, she knew it was her son Jerry.

Five months later, at Sam's family's Christmas gathering Jerry's twenty year old son approached me. He wanted to meet with me later to talk about his dad. He thought that I might be able to answer his questions since I worked for Hospice during this time.

After asking his mom if she was comfortable with us meeting, we chose a local Mexican restaurant to talk. Once Jeremy and I sat down he began telling me that he was seeing his dad in their den almost every day since the funeral. Below you will find Jeremy's account:

"I often see my father sitting in his favorite spot on the end of the sofa. I cannot understand why he is not wearing the suit that he was buried in. He has on the clothes he normally wore around the house, which were a T-shirt and a pair of jeans. He is wearing my Boy Scout pin, the one I pinned on him right before they closed his casket. He has tried several times to communicate with me, but when he moves his mouth I cannot hear him."

I did my best to answer all his questions. I explained that when we die, for the most part we communicate telepathically. I knew this from interviews with the families of the deceased, along with my own experiences. I ended our conversation, urging him to tell his dad that he and his mom will be fine... that it was o.k. to cross over. I added for him to pray that God would help him in this transition.

Author's note:

I believe that Jerry had lingered behind due to worrying about his son being left without a father for guidance. We no longer receive visits from Jerry, but I often pass by a forest that Jerry once hunted in. A smile crosses my face each time my route takes me that way. Memories of his many humorous hunting stories come flooding back to me.

Encountering Jesus

When I was thirteen years old I retired to my bed one evening, but do not recall falling to sleep. By way of a vision or a dream-like state I traveled to a place with a great open space. There were hundreds of people as far as I could see seated, separated by rows. They appeared to be waiting for a grand event to take place within a large outdoor amphitheater. There seemed to be no end to the vast multitudes of people.

While scanning the crowd I wondered why everyone was here. There was a reverent silence... an anticipation among all who were present. Everyone was standing and looking straight ahead. As I made my way across my row to the last seat Jesus came floating towards me. Instantly, I fell to my knees, but could not lift my face higher than his waist. A white halo of light surrounded him. Words could not describe what I felt.

When he reached me he laid his right hand upon my head and stated, "You are saved, and I will be with you always." He then blessed me. It was then that I became aware that I was back in my room. Tears spilled down my cheeks, as my soul filled up with sheer joy. Even now, when I share this story with anyone the tears still flow.

Author's note:

Robin did not remember going to sleep, for she most likely traveled there "in spirit." As we sleep, or as the body relaxes it appears that there are times that our spirits leave our bodies to travel to the other side, and to unknown places. There have been accounts that people have shared of traveling "in spirit" to places within the United States and across the continent.

Jonah's Message

Although, Joe and I only saw each other once a year at an annual convention, we became close friends. Each year we looked forward to exchanging family news and updated photos of our children. I remember one convention to be quite somber for Joe. His young son Jonah had recently died of cancer. As he shared his sorrow with me I thought of my own son back home. I left the conference with a heavy heart that year.

Upon returning home I decided to take my son to a local park. As I sat watching my son and other children playing, a young boy ran up to me. "Hi, my name is Jonah. Please tell my parents that I'm OK." He then ran into the woods. Stunned, I asked the other parents around me if they knew who this little boy belonged to. No one knew what child I was speaking of.

My efforts turned up futile as I searched the near-by woods with my son for over an hour. I then remembered that Joe's son was also named Jonah, and he looked just like the photo he had shown me.

After arriving home with my son, I quickly looked up Joe's number and dialed it. When I related the story to my friend he wanted me to repeat it to his wife on the other extension. I gave her a complete description of the child that had run up to me. Joe's wife was so excited that she asked for a meeting of our families to take place at my home.

Our families met for the first time and Joe's wife finally received the peace she had been praying for. She shared with me that she had been asking God for a sign that her son was safe and happy. She could now move forward with her life, knowing that her son was in a good place.

Author's note:

Through our prayers our deceased loved ones are aware when we are having a difficult time. They know that our grief, our self-imposed guilt, and our fears bind us in moving forward. These emotions keep us from completing our missions here. Our deceased loved ones know this, and wish to help us by way of giving us closure. Some come to us by way of a dream, in person, or by giving their message to another, to in turn give to us.

Through the Eyes of a Child

One day my sister and her husband heard my five year old niece Ashley, upstairs having a conversation with someone. They softly tip-toed to the second floor, stopping at her bedroom door. Their daughter was so engrossed in a conversation with an unseen visitor that she did not notice her parents observing her from the open doorway. They noted that she was sitting on her bed, looking up as if seeing someone standing in front of her.

After Ashley ended her conversation with her invisible friend they asked her whom she had been conversing with. She had quickly replied, "Poo Poo," referring to the nickname Ashley had given to one of her grandfathers, who had passed away a few months prior to this. Upon further questioning, Ashley had insisted that he had visited her. She even went as far as to say that he had dropped in to see how she was doing.

Author's note:

It has been said that children are more likely to see spirits and angels, for their minds have yet to be filled up with the everyday clutter that we accumulate each day.

Friends to the End

Alex and Timmy had been inseparable growing up. They were the best of friends and shared everything with one another. If you saw Alex you can bet Timmy was not far behind. At the age of eleven Timmy began his battle with cancer. For almost a year Alex could only stand on the sidelines as he watched Timmy's life slowly ebb away. This was not easy for young Alex to understand why this was happening to his close friend. Timmy soon died, leaving Alex lonely and confused.

Several weeks later, Alex was riding his bike when an oncoming car struck his bike, sending his body hurling through the air. As he lay in his hospital bed, having succumbed to a coma, it appeared that he had little chance of surviving. However, his mother never gave up hope. She asked friends, family, and even strangers to pray for her son. Alex's mother rarely gave up her vigil, staying days and nights for many weeks in Alex's room.

One morning she was sitting by his bedside when suddenly Alex opened his eyes. With a heart full of joy his mother shouted, "Thank God, you're going to be alright." "I know Mom, because Timmy is here with me now and he told me before you came into my room that I will be OK."

Several days later Alex was released from the hospital. He continues to live a normal life with no side effects from his accident.

A Visit From Beyond

Michael was my younger brother. At the age of fourteen he began to stay out of school, stating that he did not feel well. Our family thought he was not really sick, because he had been to numerous physicians, all who stated that he only had a sinus infection. I ribbed him constantly about skipping school, thinking that he was making up his symptoms to stay out of classes. Then something tragic happened. My brother died. The autopsy revealed that his sinus infection had gone to his brain. His illness was so rare that only a few cases had been reported within the United States.

I was devastated, sinking into a deep depression, so much so that I came close to a nervous breakdown. I blamed myself for not believing he was seriously ill. At the age of nineteen I married and had two children. Years passed by and my guilt continued to follow me. I yearned for a chance to tell my brother that I was so sorry for my actions.

One late night, after going to bed my prayers were answered. In a dreamlike state I heard someone knocking at the front door, so I got out of bed to see who it might be. When I opened the door, there stood my younger brother. I invited him in and asked him to make himself comfortable on the sofa. My bedroom was in full view of my den, and I remember glancing back at my bed where my body still lay. I then turned my full attention to my brother who was patiently waiting for me. "You need to stop worrying about me and the past. I am extremely happy where I am," stated Michael.

I was full of questions, and asked him if it hurt to die. Michael replied, "No, not at all. Would you like to see what it feels like?" As soon as I said "Yes," a tunnel opened up within the room. He

then took my hand and we traveled upwards through the tunnel at a fast rate of speed. Abruptly, we stopped to walk into a large room. It was vacant, except for a pedestal stand where a bible lay opened. I could hear the faint sounds of music and the room was filled with a soft glowing light. This place gave me a feeling of peace and the guilt that I had been carrying around for all those years melted away.

He then asked, "Now did that hurt?" I told him that it did not and begged him to take me with him. "It is not your time yet, I must take you back," my brother replied. We came back through the tunnel and once again, were sitting on the sofa. Within minutes we were saying good-by, with Michael departing by way of the front door. I then walked into my bedroom and somehow got back into my body. The next morning I was elated, knowing that it had been far more than a mere dream.

Author's note:

There are individuals who believe that there are times when our spirits leave our bodies and travel to other places. This tends to happen more at night, when we relax or fall asleep. It has been documented that individuals remember later, details about a town that they visited, while others have traveled to other continents and even to Heaven.

A Father's Love

I mentally prepared myself for my father's evitable death as I watched him fight for his life. For several weeks I had tried to bring him some form of comfort as he lay dying of cancer. I felt so fortunate that he had been alert enough to converse with me until the very end. After his passing he began visiting me in the middle of the night. He would sit on my bed each night and our conversations would center on family matters.

One occasion he told of being at his own funeral. He thought it quite humorous that anyone would grieve over his empty body. I even felt him elbow me as he laughed about family and friends viewing his body. My father stated that he was healthy and extremely happy where he was. He then became serious and apologized for not accepting my boyfriend. I told him that I understood.

I began noticing that in these visitations my father was wearing a long sleeve, blue jumpsuit. The fabric was unlike anything I've ever seen and this jumpsuit did not wrinkle when he moved. His face was tanned and he had a full head of wavy black hair. Before his death, his hair had started thinning and turning gray. He looked much younger than his sixty-some years. In fact, he looked as though he were in his thirty's.

On each visit my dad related events that were taking place in my life as well as my mother's. He would reveal what the outcome would be for whatever might be taking place. I was amazed when he told me about an ongoing insurance claim being denied. I had been injured while attending an aerobics class and my insurance company had indicated that they were denying my claim. He went on to say that they would change their decision and

that I would be receiving a check in the mail very soon, which I did after appealing my case.

One night my five-year-old niece stayed overnight due to my sister being admitted to the hospital. I lived in a one-bedroom apartment, so I let Ashley have my bed. I had another dream that night about my father as I slept on a pallet in the den. The next morning my niece asked me whom I had been talking too. I explained that I had been dreaming of my Dad. Ashley accepted my answer and continued to play.

Several months passed and my father stopped appearing in the middle of the night. Due to my busy life and worrying about my finances, I had not thought of Dad as often. My last message from my father came in a most unusual way. One late afternoon, I listened to my recorded messages and Dad's voice said, "Kathy, please call me." There had not been any old messages from my father, so I was amazed when his voice came across my answering machine. I kept the tape as a remembrance of my father.

Author's note:

Kathy shared with me that she felt her father could not communicate anymore due to her mind being so full of everyday challenges. This is why meditation and prayer are so important in our lives. If our minds are consumed with what we must do tomorrow, or if we allow fear to stand in the way it is difficult for messages to come through.

Helen's Message

Helen was one of my Hospice volunteers. One day she shared the following story with me. "One month I found myself going through an extremely rough time. The challenges in my life seemed insurmountable. During this particular time I retired one evening to bed and fell into a deep sleep. I was awakened around midnight to the sound of coins jiggling.

As I managed to open my eyes, I looked towards my bedroom doorway. There stood my deceased husband, smiling at me as he jiggled his change in his pants pocket. In life, he had a habit of doing the same thing. Several years earlier, he had lost his life due to cancer.

I was not afraid and was happy to see him. Once he knew he had my attention, he walked over to my bed, leaned down and kissed me on my forward. He then said, "Darling, everything is going to be alright." Once those words were spoken he vanished in thin air. His visit gave me the peace and the strength I needed to go through that trying time in my life. It was nice to know that he cared enough to cross over when I needed him the most.

A Visit From God

The year was 1980 and I was 32 years old. We lived in a quiet neighborhood at the end of a development. The neighborhood often held block parties and we became friends with four couples that I'm still in touch with. Our neighbors often shared stories of strange experiences within the homes at the end of our street. Our residence was no exception.

Years later, after moving to a new neighborhood only a mile away I learned that some children had unearthed proof that Native American Indians had once lived near the home we had moved from.

While living in our old neighborhood I would sometimes see a red ball of light travel around our bedroom late at night. When this happened, I made it a point to note that there were no cars turning around within the cul-de-sec at the time the light would appear.

The most horrifying experience was falling asleep many nights, and having the same reoccurring dream, of heavy footsteps quickly coming up our basement steps. Then this unknown entity would open the basement door, walk down our long hallway and stand over me on my side of the bed. I can still remember being terrified as I woke up, praying for it to go away. I could never gather enough courage to open my eyes. Later in life, I realized that this was a wandering spirit and that it was not a dream.

It was during this time that my husband had a habit of rising at dawn, two or three days a week, to go fishing at a near-by stocked pond. Upon waking one early morning, I thought my husband was standing in front of his armoire, preparing to go fishing. The security light from the neighbor's house was casting

a soft light across our bedroom floor. As my eyes began to focus, the white fabric I was seeing began to take on the form of a man. He looked to be about 5'11 inches tall. This made me sit up, while leaning on my left elbow.

He was wearing a white robe cinched with a golden girth at his waist. His robe rose high, covering his neck. He wore a highly ornate, rounded, wooden mask that covered his entire head. As I observed his jeweled head dress, the word that came to mind was "royalty." There were openings cut out for his eyes and nose and I remember that his eyes appeared to be a warm brown in color.

While sitting up in bed, I pinched myself to make sure that this was not a dream. Then the room filled up with this wonderful feeling, known as "love." How does one describe this? It is not a sense that we're familiar with here in this realm. Yes, we can feel love for one another, but not love filling every particle of breathing space. I realized that this supernatural, powerful being was there to tell me telepathically that he loved me unconditionally. I felt no fear of his mystic and strong stature. He stayed no more than a minute or two, but he left behind a sense of love, peace, and protectiveness. He had slowly formed, but departed within a blink of the eyes. Immediately, I woke my husband and told him about my visitor.

I've often wished that God would visit me again, for it was such an overwhelming experience. The thought later came to me, that he had cared enough to come at a time that this reoccurring nightmare... this surreal experience was taking place.

There have been numerous documented accounts of individuals seeing Jesus. In these documentations the person receiving a visitation is allowed to see the features of the entity that appears. In G. Scott Sparrow's book entitled, "I Am with You Always," she includes various accounts of seeing Jesus.[21] However, the bible states that no man can look upon God's face and live. In other words, our human eyes cannot take his brightness. This scripture confirms it for me, knowing that everything, but his eyes were covered.

PART FOUR

ANGELS OF THE EARTH AND AIR

"The cycle of our lives are meant to last but a moment in time, on this place we call "Earth." So for every word spoken... and with each kind or unkind deed done... it is recorded by our angels. All of these parts that we play, count toward our spiritual growth. Like dominos set-up in a circle, once started and tipped over... both good and bad acts take on a rippling effect... coming back around to teach us much about ourselves and others."

...Glenda Smith Walters

It appears that angels are celestial beings assigned to watch over us from the moment of conception. They are large in stature, but can transform themselves down to human size. Angels may appear in human form, with or without wings, or as a bright light. You may only sense their presence... hear their voice... or feel their hands guiding you out of harm's way. They are referred to in the Bible as "A Flaming Fire," (Psalms 104:4, Hebrews 1:7) "The Morning Stars" in Heaven, (Job 38:7) or "Spirits" (Hebrews 1:14).

The book of Revelation 5:11 states there are ten thousand times ten thousand, and thousands of thousands. In other words, there are more than one hundred million angels on earth and in heaven combined! Angels have been by our side since the beginning of time, and yet we are often unaware of these guests. They are God's gift of protection and guidance to us all.

The AP-GfK Poll conducted a survey with 1,000 individuals in December of 2011, asking the question, "Do you believe in Angels?" Based on these interviews 77 percent of adults stated that they believe these ethereal beings to be real.[22.]

Our Hospice patients often related seeing angels one to three weeks before they crossed over. Within the dying process, there have been individuals who related seeing two angels. After conducting numerous interviews I have come to the conclusion that one is our guardian angel and the other to be the "*Angel of Death.*"

However, patients stated that this angel was not a dark shrouded being with a sickle. Instead they recanted that the angel was more like Andrew (played by John Dye, deceased), in the now cancelled show "Touched by an Angel."[2] It appears that

this beautiful and caring angel comes at an appointed time to assist us in our transition between life and death.

In the Hindu religion, they believe that our spirits... our souls are connected to our physical bodies by a long silken cord. It is their belief that the "*Angel of Death*" severs this cord at the time our spirits are ready to cross over.

It's evident that God already knows what we need before we make our requests. The prayers of others praying for us, along with our faith appear to be key factors in releasing more angels to act upon the need at hand. Your prayers and/or the prayers of others praying for you places God's universal law into motion. Heart-felt prayers summon angels to advance and to gain strength while operating in this realm.

An Angel Watches Over Her

After arriving home from The Mayo Clinic my parents wanted to come out for a visit. I was exhausted from going through two days of extensive tests, so I opted not to go out for lunch with them. Ted, my husband was working, so I assured my parents that everything would be fine. After grocery shopping my parents stopped at Hardees, where they ran into our friends, the Carters. I was resting in bed when my mother called to see if I felt up to a visit from Rev. Carter and his wife.

I agreed to see them and asked that they give me enough time to change clothes before they arrived. After dressing with great difficulty I propped myself up with pillows on the downstairs sofa and waited for everyone to show up. Suddenly, I felt ill, so I asked God to watch over me. Luckily, by the time the Carter's and my family arrived, my nausea had subsided.

My stepfather was the first to walk into the house. I found it quite odd when he turned towards the wing chair across from me, smiled and nodded as though someone were sitting there. After briefly speaking to me he walked into the next room. By this time, everyone had come into the house. Within minutes, my stepfather came back into the den to join everyone, and inquired about my friend. He wanted to know why she had left so soon. I told him that there had been no one here but me. That's when Rev. Carter laughed and stated, "Boyd, you just met Rochella's angel."

Emergency

Early one cold wintry morning I took my husband to the emergency room at a local hospital. Once inside the lobby, an attendant whisked him away, leaving me to fill out the proper paperwork. After completing the mandated forms, the busy receptionist left without a word. Scanning the room, I noticed the many homeless people and drug addicts sleeping in the lobby chairs, trying to escape the harsh winter weather. Glancing at my watch, I noted that it was one o'clock in the morning. I then quickly chose one of two unoccupied seats facing the glass doors.

Fear took over as two men cast hostile stares my way. Suddenly, they eyed my pocketbook and started in my direction. I decided to stay put since the route to my husband would have me walking past these men. I knew only to pray for protection. No sooner had my prayer been said, than a middle-aged gentleman came through the ER entrance, carrying a large book under his arm. He wore a look of fatherly concern as his eyes met mine. His attire consisted of a colorful plaid shirt and starched khaki pants.

To my surprise he walked directly towards me, without glancing around the room. As he reached my chair, he asked if the adjacent seat was taken. I eagerly responded by saying, "No, please feel free to sit down." I went on to express my prior uneasiness. Thanks to this stranger, the menacing men who had started walking my way hastily returned to their seats.

As we conversed, I learned that he was there to check out his wife. For some odd reason, it did not occur to me at the time, that doctors do not release patients this early in the morning.

I noticed that he carried a book by the great mystery writer, Agatha Christie. It was entitled, "Hercule Poirot's Casebook."[23] This particular book intrigued me, because as a child, I had read

books by Trixie Belden,[24] Nancy Drew,[25] and The Hardy Boys. My numbered series of Nancy Drew books had been my absolute favorites. In fact, I loved books so much that I rarely played with dolls. I often fashioned myself as Nancy Drew, looking for secret passageways in my grandmother's upstairs closets.

His presence and soft-spoken voice had quite a calming effect on me. Almost an hour had passed when he stood up, announcing, "It is time for me to go." In fact, he stated this twice as I desperately tried to find out more about him. His twinkling blue eyes seemed to be withholding a secret that he could not share.

This benevolent entity insisted that his book was now mine. He refused my offer of payment stating, "I've read all I need to. The book is for you." He carefully placed the thick hardback in my hands and walked towards the automated glass doors. The first set of doors opened as he continued walking toward the last set of exit doors.

It was at this moment I noticed the attendant wheeling my husband out into the lobby. Quickly, I glanced back to my departing visitor, who by now should have been walking through the second set of doors. The parking lot was well lit and the glass doors were closed, but he was no-where in sight. It was as if his departure had been timed precisely.

Months passed before it dawned on me that hospitals do not check patients out in the evening or the wee hours of the morning. Upon checking with this same hospital, they verified that patients are released between the hours of 8 a.m. and 12 noon. Also, this gentleman's wife had never appeared in the waiting room, nor were any cars seen coming or going. The spacious emergency entrance was made of glass from the ceiling to the floor. Anyone entering or exiting could easily have been seen. There can be no other explanation than this was my guardian angel. His gift now rests among my treasured collection of Nancy Drew books.

Author's note:

This story aired on "This Strange Universe" in April of '97. This show was produced out of Burbank, California, 1996-1997 by Rusher Entertainment, and it was created by Paul Barrosse.[26] This story later appeared, within the same year on Channel 8 Fox News (WGHP).[27.]

A Parting Foretold

My mother is a woman of great courage and strength. She contracted TB, was quarantined, and placed in a sanatorium when I was a mere child. For two years, my Dad faithfully took my younger sister and me each week to see her. She was only allowed to view us from an upstairs window as we stood in the sanatorium's parking lot.

I can still remember looking up as she smiled and waved to us below. I've often thought how hard it must have been for my mother not to be able to hug us for two long years. Only when she arrived home, did I learn of her angelic visitor, and how that visit prepared her for what was to come.

Mother stated that a month before she became ill, an angel had appeared late one night at the foot of her bed. She described him as the most beautiful being she had ever seen. She asked him why he was there. He had replied, "I'm your guardian angel, and I have been sent to tell you to spend as much time as you can with your children, because soon you will be separated. Think of all the times that you lost your patience with them, the times you were too busy to make time to be together. Be aware of this, so that you will live within the moment." She then shared that she had replied, "But if you're an angel, then why do you not have wings?"

My Mom smiled as she told of how the angel had crossed his massive arms across his broad chest, while bursting into laughter at her remark. He then exclaimed, "I can appear with or without them, or however you perceive me to be." With his last statement, she said, he then smiled and slowly faded away.

I now understand how the angel's message had given my mother the hope and the courage she needed to hang on for those two years.

The Warning

One evening, on my way home from work, I pulled my car into a local convenience store to fuel up. After pumping the gas and paying with a credit card at an outside window, I noticed a man lurking in the shadows. He was wearing a toboggan with a dark windbreaker pulled up around his neck. His hands were shoved deep into his pockets. I thought his attire was rather odd since the night air was quite warm.

I had planned to go inside the store to purchase a soft drink, but could not shake the feeling that something was not quite right. While walking around my car, a disembodied voice warned, "Do not walk in front of that man... leave now." Other than the attendant within the glass booth, no one else was in the parking lot. I decided to adhere to the voice's warning and left. I believe that an angel saved me from being robbed, attacked, or from something far worse that fateful night.

Payment Overdue

One of my past positions placed me serving as a Collection Manager for a local furniture company. There was one customer whom I'll never forget. This particular client had a business and a personal account. Her personal account was paid in full, but her business account was past due. Unfortunately, she refused to acknowledge her billing statements, along with my phone calls. After sending several collection letters and leaving urgent messages on her answering machine I turned the matter over to the company's attorney.

The attorney's assistant (Ann) called during this time to inform me that this woman was impossible to work with. She went as far as to state that she must be possessed, because each time she spoke with her on the phone, her body would shake with fear. While we were conversing, I heard a woman ask for me in the next room. Only the staff was allowed upstairs, so I was surprised when this same stranger was now standing in my office doorway. Immediately, my body began shaking uncontrollably. I told Ann that this woman was now in my office and asked her to pray for me, thus ending our conversation.

My attention was now drawn to the highly agitated woman charging towards me. My four co-workers could only stand frozen in place. It was apparent to me that she was going to cause me physical harm. My instincts sensed a dark presence around her. Her ranting became louder as she advanced... her eyes glaring like a wild animal. Suddenly, she came to a halt, stopping within a few feet of where I stood. It was as if there was an invisible wall... an invisible force standing between the two of us. She appeared frightened as she quickly handed me a statement, showing her personal account paid in full.

I found it strange that she had extended her right arm out and around some invisible entity. In order to perform this act, she had leaned forward on her toes to reach me. She was too upset to allow me to explain that her business account was the account that was past due. The woman then turned on her heels and fled, leaving everyone to wonder what had just taken place.

Fortunately, for Ann and myself, the attorney was able to deal with this woman's husband and the bill was settled. There is no doubt in my mind that an angel had stood in front of me that day, protecting me. The woman's frightened expression was proof enough.

An Angel Saves the Day

Opening up my new hair salon was a real challenge for me. As a single parent back then, it had taken every penny I had to open the doors. On the first day, several stylists were working on clients while some customers were under the dryers reading magazines. Then the unexpected happened... the power went out. My hairdressers were frantic, and the customers were worried about not being able to meet prior commitments. Everyone started milling around and talking with one another.

I frantically went door to door, checking with other shop owners, but they had power. After relating my dilemma to the artist that was stenciling my windows, he left to find his brother who was an electrician. I decided to check the fuses in the back room and panicked when the fuses looked to be fine. I decided then and there to call upon a higher source to send someone who could help me.

Within minutes there was a knock at the back door. I swung open the heavy door, and there stood this nice looking young man. He was dressed in a dark brown suit, white shirt, sporting a mint green tie. His hair was dark auburn, and his clear blue eyes sparkled. My first thought was that this was the artist's brother, but wondered why he was wearing a suit. He smiled and said, "I understand you need some help." I asked if he meant with my electricity. He replied, "Yes," and walked over to my fuse box.

It took him only a few minutes to restore the power and the dryers came back on. Needless to say, I was elated and asked how much the bill was. "Nothing, I was sent to help you," he stated. With that he walked out the same door he had entered earlier. By this time, the stencil artist had returned to tell me

that his brother was not at home. I explained what had transpired and described the young man in detail. He said that his brother did not fit this description.

My shop was located in a small rural town, where everyone knew each other, so I began asking the local townspeople who they thought might have showed up at my back door that day. It turned out that no one matched his description and none of the operators or clients had seen him in the salon that day. Thanks to an answered prayer and an angel, my business was spared.

Angel Behind the Wheel

Snow had begun to fall as I set out with my mother-in-law to pick up my youngest daughter Christy at school. After retrieving my daughter, we started out for home. By this time the snow turned into sleet, and I was forced to slowly inch my way forward. Suddenly, my car hit an icy spot, spinning us around in the road. Gripping the wheel tighter I sent up a silent prayer.

Within minutes, an approaching car with two large men inside pulled up. The passenger asked if he could be of assistance, so I asked if he would drive us home. Normally, I would have been too frightened to allow a stranger in my car, but the road conditions frightened me far more. To my relief, he instructed his friend to follow us and climbed into the driver's seat. On the way home, we each chatted with the stranger as if we were old friends. The stranger had such a warm personality that he put all of us at ease.

Once we arrived at my house, we exchanged names and I asked him for his phone number. He stated his name, and that he was listed in the local phone book. I thanked him as he got out of my car and handed me the keys. We became concerned when we noticed that the other driver was no longer behind us. I then told him that my next-door neighbor might be able to give him a lift. The stranger insisted on walking and started up our driveway.

When he reached the mailbox he started sprinting up the road. We watched as he topped the hill; he just simply vanished without a trace. My mother-in-law and daughter looked up and down the road, but could not even find his footprints in the snow. In the meantime, I went inside to look up his name in the phone book, only to find that he was not listed.

The Lost Keys

My family and I were spending a week at Myrtle Beach, South Carolina, when we had a rather unusual incident take place. Larry and I spent the day on the beach and as we were packing up to go back to the condo, he realized his keys were missing. He thought he had placed them in the beach bag, but after checking, they were not there. My youngest daughter was watching her older sister make sandwiches for our lunch, when my husband Larry and I came in from the beach.

Upon entering the beach house he asked our daughters if they had seen his keys and they had not. He frantically began checking our bags and retracing his steps. He decided to go back to the beach and ask if anyone had found any keys. After several hours he came back empty-handed. By this time he was starting to panic and began calling around to see how he could replace the lost keys.

I told him not to worry, that as a family we would pray about it. Within minutes of praying, a young woman with a child showed up at our front door. The stranger stated that her daughter had found some keys in the surf as she was wading, and wondered if they might be ours. I recognized our keys as she handed them to me. I turned to give them to my husband and when I turned back to face the door, the mother and her daughter were gone. My husband could not understand how they had known which condo to come to. However, I knew how and who had sent them.

The Good Samaritan

My partner, Cindy, and I once owned a chimney sweep business. We wore the top hats, the tails, and the whole works. Cindy, her son Ty, and I were on our way to an early morning appointment when we had a flat tire. We managed to roll to a stop near a high school that had been closed for the summer.

As we assessed our situation, we realized neither of us knew how to change a tire. We decided to go as far as pulling out a mat and the spare tire from the back of the van, placing it on the ground beside the flat tire. After surveying the area, there appeared to be no one home at any of the near-by houses. With no phone, a closed schoolhouse, and unoccupied homes, we knew that we would have no choice, but to walk many miles to obtain help.

We were still discussing what we should do when a car appeared around the curve and pulled up beside our van. I noticed that this young man was wearing a plaid shirt and tan pants. He appeared to stand just less than six feet tall. Without a word, he got out of his car, walked around the van and started changing the tire. As the three of us stood back watching, I turned to Ty, (Cindy's son) and exclaimed, "See, Ty, there really are angels." Before the flat, we had been discussing how angels guide, protect and help us throughout our life. The stranger looked over his shoulder, smiled and gave us a knowing nod. With his task finished, he got into his car and sped away. He had changed the tire without saying one word to us.

We piled back into the van and began discussing the possibility that this had been an angel in disguise. After all, how had he known we had a flat? From the road he could not have seen that we had a flat due to the way we had parked the van.

I quickly turned the van around to catch up to him, accelerating to sixty. There were no cars on the road, and we found no parked cars that fit the description of his in the near-by driveways. I've often wondered if this "Good Samaritan" was an angel in disguise.

Author's note:

This story aired on "This Strange Universe." This show was produced out of Burbank, California in April of 1996-1997 by Rusher Entertainment, and it was created by Paul Barrosse.[26]

Harry's Close Call

I always took great pride in my yard and could not understand why my neighbor could care less about how his property looked. He continued to bring home old dilapidated cars, placing his finds on his front lawn. The beautiful lake view that we once enjoyed was now blocked by my neighbor's junk. One day, while mowing I became so over-wrought with my neighbor's unkempt yard that I was fuming to myself. The more I thought about it the madder I became.

I did not notice the steep incline that was looming up ahead. Time seemed to slow down as my riding lawnmower flipped over, pinning me face up on the ground. Immediately, I felt two strong hands grab me under my arms, sliding me out from under the mower. This unseen force then threw me away from the mower. Fortunately, my wife had been sitting outside in a near-by chair. She came running up the knoll when she saw the mower flip. She found me lying face down in a nearby gully. My wife helped me to my feet and asked how I ended up in the ditch. I told her that an angel had pulled me out from under the overturned mower.

Upon standing, I noticed that the motor was still running. It was then that the full impact hit me. Thanks to my guardian angel, I was able to walk away from the accident without a scratch. I decided then and there, that it might be in my best interest to control my thoughts and bad temper in the future.

A Road Trip To Be Remembered

I use to be a Navy fighter pilot during the Vietnam War. I flew F6F'S, F4F'S, F4B4'S, F4U'S, SOC'S, and O52U'S. In fact, at that time there was not a plane that I had not flown for the Navy. I also drove tractor trailers for several years. After retiring I bought a camper and toured the United States with my wife Pat. We took many long adventurous vacations together.

On this one particular trip, we were on our way to Salisbury, Maryland. As we traveled down a freeway in Eland, North Carolina, pulling our camper behind us, a semi-tractor trailer sideswiped us. Instantly, I could see someone in my rearview mirror, dressed in a light brown robe, standing behind my seat. His attire reminded me of what one would wear in Biblical days. It baffled me how anyone could stand in such cramped quarters. I can still remember the sweet scent of lilacs that surrounded me that day.

In a calm voice the man said, "Pat it will be all right. Do what you know to do and do it now!" In truck driving school we were taught how to make a semi-tractor jack-knife, so that the rig would cause fewer accidents. Upon hearing his voice, I hoped that my Ford pick-up and camper might respond in the same manner.

I turned the camper brakes off and locked the truck's brakes up. This caused my Ford F250 truck to respond by jack-knifing and toppling over, avoiding the bridge abutment that loomed ahead. The first person to arrive on the scene was Mr. Walters, a minister from Durham. Pulling with all his might he could not wrench my truck door open. I tried to push from the inside as well, but to no avail.

After many futile attempts, Mr. Walters stopped to rest. It was then that the door popped open and he was able to pull my wife out. He told me later that he had not been the one who opened the door. The local firemen tested the truck door, and to all of our astonishment it would not close. Once again my angel had come to my rescue.

Author's note:

Harry Spanglar was interviewed in Lexington, NC by a High Point, NC crew, sent out by "This Strange Universe" in April of '97.[26] This show was produced out of Burbank, California, 1996-1997 by Rusher Entertainment, and created by Paul Barrosse.

Angels Watching Over Me

After sending my youngest son off to college, I decided to spend the winter in Florida with my daughter. Most of my possessions were sold and given away, in order to purchase a motor home. My trip took me through several states, with many nights being spent in well-lit parking lots at trucking plazas.

One evening, I felt uneasy about being alone and pulled my RV under a security light at a large truck stop. After bedding down for the evening I asked God to send angels to protect me. I first thought it was a dream, when I awoke to whispers within my RV.

As my eyes began to focus, I viewed several large beings sitting at my kitchen table, while some were in the driver and passenger seats. They appeared to be conversing with one another in low tones, so they would not wake me. These angelic visitors were so tall they had to bend over to avoid hitting their heads on the ceiling.

Angels never frightened me, because I've experienced them many times in my life. For some reason I'm blessed in being able to see them now and then. Trying not to be disrespectful, I laughed and said, "I asked for protection, but I did not think that you would throw a party." I then turned over and fell into a deep sleep, knowing that angels were watching over me.

Author's note:

Cecile had phoned Hospice to ask about volunteering when she first moved to town. She had found a small apartment near the post office. Upon my first visit I learned that she made her living doing alterations, so I often dropped off items to be hemmed or mended. Our visits consisted of sitting in her kitchen drinking

hot tea, sharing angel stories. On one of these visits she gave me a bumper sticker that read, "Angels on Board," along with a pad depicting an angel holding a ball of light. One day I stopped by to see Cecile, only to find her apartment empty. I was quite sad to know that she had moved on. No doubt she is off on her next adventure.

Not Before Spring

Sandy and I had a long-standing friendship. When she first learned of her cancer, I was one of the few friends she told. In the spring of her second year of battling the disease, she had a spiritual experience that gave her the courage needed to face her death. Sandy called one day and asked me to come over. When I arrived, she shared that others might not believe her story due to her medication, and that is why she had only called me to come over.

As we sat in her den, she told of losing her footing one day as she descended her staircase. She felt as though she were falling forward in slow motion. According to Sandy an angel appeared... reached out and broke her fall, catching her in mid-air. She stated that after the angel caught her he exclaimed, "It is not your time to go. Your time will come in the spring."

Sandy continued, sharing another incident that had taken place two weeks later. On this particular day she told of how her illness had totally drained her to the point of exhaustion, so she took a long nap on the sofa. The following depicts what she shared with me on that day. Upon waking, she noticed the same angel sitting in a nearby chair observing her. The angel then told her to look out the window and to tell him what she saw. She was speechless due to having a hard time comprehending the miracle she was viewing from her den window.

Sandy went on to say that snowflakes were floating slowly to the ground, and yet it was late spring. Just an hour earlier, the sun had been out. Her outdoor thermometer had shown an earlier reading in the high eighties. The angel then stated that this was being shown to Sandy to let her know that it was not yet her spring... in other words it was not her time to cross over. After he

told her this he faded away. Seeing the snow and the angel had made her death easier to accept. She felt at peace for the first time since learning of her health problems.

"I want to leave this story behind for you to share with others... to give them hope of our life beyond this realm. Do not repeat this story until after I have gone," stated Sandy. It gave me a sense of peace that my friend had entrusted me with a message to give to others.

Two weeks later, the phone call I had been dreading came. Sandy had crossed over in the spring of her life. At first, I was saddened by my loss. Then I remembered the special gift she had left behind... a gift that could be shared and passed on to others who needed to hear her story.

Kicking the Habit

Over the years I had tried many times to kick my smoking habit. I would quit for a while only to light one up again within a few weeks. Finally, I decided to ask God to take away my craving for cigarettes forever. As I sat with my daughter in a local restaurant, enjoying a bowl of soup, I could not resist lighting up once more.

Suddenly, we watched in disbelief as my cigarette flew out from between my fingers, traveling upwards and then diving flame first into my soup. It was as if some invisible hand had seized it from my fingers and dropped it into the hot liquid. We were stunned for several minutes. When we were able to speak, my daughter asked me how this could have happened. I can only assume that my angel helped me out. This incident shook me up enough to kick the habit. To this day I do not smoke and I'm allergic to cigarette smoke.

My Name Is Barry

While my tire was being repaired, I decided to browse next door at the local automotive shop. The first items my eyes took in were a stack of white, miniature Gideon Bibles, stacked neatly by the cash register. Although, there was one at home I decided to take another one.

It was two weeks before Christmas and visions of upcoming events played out in my head. I could not understand why as a family, we could not simplify our gift giving, experiencing the true meaning of Christmas. For some reason the season always brought me sorrow instead of joy. Due to the attitude of one member of my family, this person always put a damper on our festivities. But how does one convince family members to break years of tradition? How could we find a way to come together as a loving family and have a joyful time? I soon became tired of browsing and decided to sit outside the body shop to wait.

Looking up the road, I noticed a young man who appeared to be homeless, carrying a heavy bedroll slung over one sagging shoulder. His outcast garments hung on his thin frame, and his scuffed up shoes were far too big for his feet. He crossed the road and walked in front of me without a backwards glance. The man carefully laid down his backpack at the shop's front door and entered the building. At this moment the technician let me know that he had finished putting my tire back on. Trying not to stare at this young man, I paid the mechanic and thanked him.

While starting my car, this inner voice urged me to give this homeless man the small Bible; along with what-ever money was in my purse. The lone ten-dollar bill looked quite forlorn in my wallet. This was all the money I had to hold me until payday. I'm sorry to say that my first thought was to resist due to fear.

During the ongoing debate between the inner voice and my conscious, the man came out of the store, picked up his bedroll and quickly crossed the road.

I knew that time was running out and that the test had been laid out before me. Minutes ticked by as I tried to make the right decision. Trusting that inner voice, I jumped into my car and drove up the busy street. A lone dirt road loomed up ahead, that would place me several yards ahead of the stranger. I turned onto the dusty road and got out of my car. This placed me directly in the stranger's path. Facing each other I chimed, "Merry Christmas," while handing him the miniature Bible with the ten dollar bill pressed between the pages.

"Hi, my name is Barry," he stated, displaying a half-toothless grin. "And my name is Linda," I replied. The twinkle in his deep blue eyes seemed so familiar. Upon a closer look, his smudged face looked quite young. A few of his teeth were missing, and when he smiled his face appeared to take on this ethereal glow. Time stood still for that one brief moment, unfolding like a Hallmark greeting card.

Once I jumped back into my car and backed out onto the main road, I stole a backward glance. Suddenly, my spirit was renewed with the true meaning of Christmas, for there was Barry walking onward on his journey, intensely reading his new Bible. He showed no interest in the money. My spirit soared as I watched his steps become lighter, and his pace pick up.

Was Barry a mere mortal who had fallen on hard times or an angel sent to test me? His sparkling blue eyes led me to believe in the latter. I later remembered seeing those same unusual eyes on another occasion. I often think of Barry around the holidays, and how he taught me the true meaning of Christmas. It is the joy of giving, not the anticipation of receiving. It is the warmth of a house to go home to... it is the love a family shares no matter what differences may occur.

Mary's Angel

Mary learned in her late thirty's that she had colon cancer. Due to her weight she thought no man would ever love her, much less marry her. She had been wrong, because a wonderful man named Fred fell in love with Mary, and they were married within a few months. Now that she had found her soul mate, she felt that life had dealt her an unfair blow.

She threw herself into her household chores, trying not to think about the day when she could no longer perform her wifely duties. Within six months of her diagnosis, Mary became bedridden, and her family took turns staying with her while Fred worked. It soon became apparent that they needed help caring for Mary, so Hospice was called in.

Mary often shared her fear of death with me. She did not want to continue to suffer, but she was afraid to let go. One day I noted that Mary seemed to be quite excited about something. She shared that she was no longer afraid to die. She began to tell of a bright light cascading down through the skylight in her bedroom.

A voice, which she said was Jesus stated, "I am leaving an angel with you so that you will no longer be afraid." Mary then went on to tell of a beautiful angel that slowly appeared under this same skylight. She giggled when she told me that her angel only disappeared when her husband entered the room. She was so elated, that she gave me permission to tell everyone.

Mary continued to share her story with anyone who would listen. Each time we changed her bed linens, Mary would let us know if we were blocking her view of the angel. She would always describe the angel's features and where she was standing in the room.

She tried many times to cross over, but her love and concern for her family constantly pulled her back. You see, Mary had always played the roles of "peacemaker" and "caregiver," so this was why it was so difficult for her to let go.

We became concerned for Mary, and sent a social worker to talk with her family members. The social worker explained to the family once again that Mary needed their permission to let go. She asked that they express their love, along with indicating that they would be fine.

Through Mary's family, our staff learned that the angel assigned to watch over her, stayed until the very end... never leaving her side. After each family member said their "good-bys", they noticed that Mary took one final glance towards the beam of light. Although, they could not see the angel standing under the skylight, they believed that Mary could. Seeing the angel had given her the courage she needed to face her passing.

Author's note:

Mary's case is one of many that prove that the spirit is stronger than the physical body. This is why Hospice believes in encouraging the family to give their dying loved ones permission to let go. This makes their transition easier for everyone.

During the thirteen years working for Hospice, I learned of patients who were in the last stages of death, hang on until their children arrived from another state. There is usually a time when they appear to feel better and are more coherent. In the last weeks of a person's life there is often an ongoing struggle between life and death... between the spirit and the physical body. It is my belief that this is a time when the spirit appears to be coming in and out of the body... testing out its spiritual surroundings.

Many Hospice families state that at the time of their loved ones' death, a feeling of peace... a kind of reverence enters the room. I believe this stillness they're referring to are angels making their presence known. It is the kind of reverence that no words are uttered or a sound is made.

Her Weight in Gold

I have wrestled with a weight problem all of my life, trying almost every diet that came along. The more depressed I became, the more food became my long-time friend. One night I broke down and begged God to show me that he loved me, weaknesses and all. That evening I cried myself to sleep. Sometime during the night, I heard an angelic voice from behind me say, "Don't worry about your weight." And then the voice came around in front of me saying, "In his time I will help you."

I then looked up and beheld this luminous golden angel standing very close to me. She was transparent with no wings and her flaxen hair hung in waves, blowing gently around her face. A bright white light illuminated her slender silhouette from behind. I studied her face, trying to etch each detail into my memory.

When my thoughts dwelt on the angel's eyes, or her nose, the angel would change the shape and size of the physical feature that I gazed upon. And each time the angel did this... like a vapor she would engulf me with this outpouring warmth... this feeling of unconditional love.

From deep within, I could feel her love overflowing into my vèry soul. To this day I have never felt such unconditional love. Words could not describe how wonderful I felt for the first time in my life. It was as if this angel was showing me that outward features were not what I should focus my attention on. Instead of focusing on my weight, she wanted me to learn to love myself and share that love with others.

"You know everything about me," I stated. The angel then responded by changing the shape of her eyes. Within minutes my golden angel disappeared, leaving me to wonder if I would

ever see her again. I'm not an artist, but I wanted to capture her delicate features on paper before my memory faded.

For three days I searched for the right color that would match the angel's brilliance. Finally, I saw it on a neon sign, while coming home from work one day. With great determination, I found the correct colored pencil and began sketching her. After my sister saw my drawing and heard my story, she was so excited that she began sharing my story with everyone.

Author's note:

Sharon ended our telephone interview, stating that she knew she had only received a small taste of what it would be like in heaven. She still struggles with her weight, but due to the angel's encouraging message, Sharon realizes that true beauty comes from within. She still yearns to see her golden angel. However, her experience has left a lasting impression by teaching her to love herself for who she is.

Angelic Encounters

Throughout my life I've had many supernatural and unexplained events take place. At a very young age, I recall something that happened during a bad bout with pneumonia. While lying in my bed one night three angels appeared floating above me. Their long blonde hair and white flowing robes billowed as a gentle breeze stirred throughout the room. A blue vaporous cloud engulfed them as they sang to me softly.

Other events took place, but only one other incident stands out in my mind. My husband and I were coming out of a church meeting one night when we discovered that our car would not start. We were quite worried, because the surrounding neighborhood was not a safe place to be in after dark. My husband asked the last few remaining individuals if they had jumper cables, but no one had any. Soon the parking lot was empty as everyone hurried home, unconcerned with the position it left us in. I knew only to start praying that someone would be sent to help us.

Within minutes, a young woman came around the corner of the building, carrying a set of cables. We hooked them up and our car started right away. My husband and I thanked her, but she merely smiled and proceeded back around the building. We wanted to be sure her car started, so we drove to the other side of the church, but we found no one.

The Strength of Angels

While vacationing with my family in Gatlinburg, Tennessee my sister and I were intrigued by a shop's sign that read, "The Jewelry Celebration," so we ventured inside. A dear lady by the name of Reva was managing her daughter's store that day. As my sister browsed, I introduced myself and began leading our conversation towards my favorite subject. Reva was more than happy to share the following angel story with me:

At the age of thirty, Gary... my son-in-law, experienced something that our family will never forget. He was working under a car when he asked his friend Steve to start the engine. Without thinking Steve failed to push the clutch in, causing the car to lunge off the ramp onto Gary's chest. The weight of the car caused his lungs to collapse. Steve ran next door, calling out to his wife to dial "911." He quickly returned with a neighbor and his two older sons. They each stood on the side of the car that Gary lay under, but the four of them could not lift the heavy vehicle.

It was at this time Steve decided to lean on his newfound faith. With a voice of authority Steve stated, "In the name of Jesus lift," and the four men tried once more to move the car off of my son-in-law. Suddenly, the car began to move upward, allowing Steve to see the bare feet of four enormous beings on the other side of the car. He realized at that moment he was in the presence of angels. With the help of his angelic friends, they were able to move the car off of Gary's body. Once the car was moved, the angels materialized before his very eyes.

The local police blocked off the traffic around Gary's house as the medic helicopter sat down. In the meantime, a doctor who worked in the trauma unit in Birmingham, Alabama was listening to his scanner at home when the "911' call came in.

He arrived at the hospital just as the medic helicopter touched down, carrying my son-in-law.

After waiting for several hours, my daughter was told by Gary's doctor that he had only a slim chance of surviving. Immediately, our families started prayer chains throughout our community. There were fifty churches praying for his recovery. My son-in-law was a choir member in his church and his doctors stated that if he survived, he would not be able to sing again. Miraculously, Gary was released from the hospital within four days and continues to sing in his church choir.

I'll never forget Reva's radiate face as she finished telling me her incredible story. My sister purchased a pair of earrings, while Reva and I exchanged telephone numbers. Before leaving for home that evening I decided to go back to the shop with my family, to say a final farewell to my newfound friend. When we walked into the shop, Reva said that she was happy that we had come back in, because she had something for me. She carefully reached into a near-by display case and pulled out a small silver Bible charm. "I thought you might like to have this. I've never seen one quite like it," she stated.

Upon opening the small clasp, I found a heavenly treasure inside. A miniature angel knelt beside a baby Jesus in a manager. My family and I look forward each year to traveling to Gatlinburg to watch their Christmas parade. Unfortunately, the shop is no longer there, but I think of Reva each time we visit that magical place. Her gift now dangles on my charm bracelet with other charms, each one bearing a story.

Author's note:

There are people with whom we only have a chance meeting, never to see again. However, their encouraging words and kind deeds will make such an impact that it will last us a lifetime. The following account is another story that Reva shared that day.

A Scripture to Hold Onto

Last year my mother learned she had colon cancer, with only three months to live. I felt so helpless watching her go through this terrible illness, knowing that she would not be with me much longer. As we were preparing to leave the hospital after one of her treatments, it began to rain. I led her to an upstairs waiting room and took the elevator down to move my car.

Once the elevator doors closed I asked God for a verse to hang onto. Suddenly, someone was standing behind me. No one had been in the elevator earlier, but upon glancing down and to my right, I saw two bare feet. I chose not to turn around, believing that I was in the presence of an angel. It was as if time slowed down, as the angel recited Psalms 91.

> *"He that dwelleth in the secret place of the most high shall abide under the shadow of the Almighty. I will say of the Lord, he is my refuge and my fortress: my God; in him will I trust. Surely, he shall deliver thee from the snare of the fowler, and from the noisome pestilence. He shall cover thee with his feathers, and under his wings shall thou trust: his truth shall be thy shield and buckler.*
>
> *Thou shalt not be afraid; nor for the arrow that flieth by day: Nor for the pestilence that walketh in darkness; nor for the destruction that wasteth at noonday. A thousand shall fall at thy side, and ten thousand at thy right hand; but it shall not come nigh thee. Only with thine eyes shalt thou behold and see the reward of the wicked. Because thou hast made the Lord, which is my refuge, even the most High,*

thy habitation; there shall no evil befall thee, neither shall any plague come nigh thy dwelling. For he shall give his angels charge over thee, to keep thee in all thy ways.

They shall bear thee up in their hands, lest thou dash thy foot against a stone. Thou shalt tread upon the lion and adder: the young lion and the dragon shalt thou trample under feet. Because he hath set his love upon me, therefore will I deliver him: I will set him on high, because he hath known my name? He shall call upon me, and I will answer him: I will be with him in trouble; I will deliver him, and honor him. With long life will I satisfy him and shew him my salvation."

When the angel had spoken the last word of scripture, the elevator doors opened, and I stepped into the lower lobby. I gathered my courage and turned around, but the elevator was empty. The angel's scripture reading gave me something to hang onto through the next few months. It helped me to remain strong for my mother in her last days.

Vicky's Angelic Encounter

Throughout my life I taught others how to spin yarn in various textile mills. The work could be grueling at times with long hours, but I've always enjoyed being around people. The rundown mill I worked in had needed repairs for many years. The freight elevator doors were so old that they consisted of rusty steel bars that slid up and down.

After one of my morning breaks I stepped into the freight elevator to go back up to my station on the second floor. I was so preoccupied having had a discussion about spiritual experiences with my co-workers that I did not notice the iron grate coming down. My head hit the gate, knocking me to the floor. My body lay inside the elevator, while my head rested in the hallway. Still dazed, I looked up to see the heavy steel grate plummeting towards my neck.

Suddenly, someone gently picked me up and placed me in the corridor. I found myself sitting up with my back to the elevator doors. My uncle, who also worked there found me on the floor and helped me up. Unfortunately, he arrived too late to see the angel who had rescued me.

A Prayer for Charles

As my little boy lay in a coma, a beautiful woman dressed in a white uniform and matching cap entered his hospital room. She told me that she had dropped by to pray for my son. I did not think of her visit as being anything but ordinary, because she was dressed like a nurse. She placed her hands on either side of my son's face and began to pray and to sing. The melody was not familiar to me, but it brought a sense of peace into the room.

After my mysterious visitor finished her song she turned towards me and said, "Your son will be fine now. He will be going home soon." She then slipped quietly out of the room, just as Charles took his last breath. Immediately, I ran out to inform a nurse that my son had stopped breathing. Earlier, I had signed a "Do Not Resuscitate" order due to the many years he had endured this illness. I did not wish to see him suffer any longer. Two nurses came into the room while I searched the hall looking for the lady in white, but the hallway was empty.

The nurse's station was located directly across the hall from my son's room, so I asked the nurses if they had seen this young woman. I gave a detailed description and explained what had taken place. Each nurse acknowledged that they had heard singing coming from the room, but had not seen anyone enter or exit my child's room. They also informed me that nurses no longer wore caps of any kind.

Author's note:

Charlie's mother had mistaken the angel's message. This is understandable since we relate home to here. The angel had been referring to his heavenly home. As strange as it may seem,

as I stated earlier, some believe in the possibility that we dwelt together in heaven "in spirit" before coming to earth. Job 38:4-7 reads, *"Where wast thou when I laid the foundations of the earth? Declare, if thou hast understanding. Who hath laid the measures thereof, if thou knowest? Or who hath stretched the line upon it? Where upon are the foundations there of fastened? Or who laid the corner stone thereof; when the morning stars (angels) sang together, and all the sons of God (us) shouted for joy?"*

Could it be that our friends, families, and those acquaintances that help us along the way, all knew one another on the other side before coming here? Have you not met at-least one complete stranger, only to feel as though you had met before? Is it not ironic how often the same friends or acquaintances appear more than once to lend us a hand... to uplift our spirits as we each travel on our separate journeys?

The Angelic Mover

My husband was offered a promotion that was too good to pass up. However, it required us to travel across the country, driving thousands of miles. Before we set out we cautiously timed our trip through the California desert for much later in the evening. In my husband's haste to leave he had failed to purchase a new spare tire. Unfortunately, half-way through our trek across the desert we had a flat tire. We both panicked, because Norm had chosen a road that was not well traveled. He thought by taking this route that he would be cutting off an hour's drive. After pulling our car and trailer off the road, we discussed whether we should wait until someone came our way. We decided to say a prayer.

Within minutes bright lights appeared in our rearview mirror. The moving van stopped just short of our trailer, and a young man jumped out of the cab. He asked if we were having trouble. My husband stated that he needed to buy a new tire, so the man offered to drive us to the closest service station.

As we rode along, Norm asked who he worked for since there was no lettering on his van. The truck driver said his name was Joe Brown, along with the company's name. We drove for an hour to reach a local garage. The station's owner then sent a wrecker out to tow our car and trailer in. We thanked the stranger and he disappeared into the night.

Weeks later my husband called the moving company that Joe worked for. He wanted to compliment them for having such caring drivers. The dispatcher told my husband that no one by that name worked for the company. We then realized that an angel had been dispatched to help us that night.

PART FIVE

DREAMS AND VISIONS

Your young men will see visions, and your old men will dream dreams.

...Acts 2:17

There is a distinct difference between dreaming, triggered by our memory banks, and dreaming in the Alpha State. This is a state of mind between being awake and asleep. You're aware of the sounds taking place around you. You may find yourself dreaming of a visit from a deceased loved one, or an event that is going to take place.

In this quiet state, you are more receptive to God's guidance and his messages. When you have entered the Alpha State, this places you to be more receptive to the spiritual realm. You are vulnerable while you sleep. Before drifting off you may wish to pray for protection as you sleep.

Goodnight Granddaddy

On August 20, 2003 my grandfather passed away at the age of ninety-one. He mowed two acres each week in the summer months, ran errands for my ailing grandmother, and attended church regularly. In my eyes he was a saint with angelic white hair. Grandfather could repair lawnmowers, sewing machines, and almost anything mechanical. He left this world doing what he loved to do most, and that was mowing his yard.

Earlier that day I had been sitting at a stoplight, and that inner voice asked, "Don't you think that you should visit your grandparents?" I had not listened, because my husband and I were leaving for Stuart, Florida that afternoon to visit friends. I justified that there was not time to drop in to see them. We were five hours into our trip when my mother called to let us know that my grandfather had died late that afternoon.

Realizing that I had been given a chance to see him one last time, I was quite upset with myself. In fact, this inner voice had spoken several times to me throughout my life. Yet, once again I had failed to listen, reasoning that it was only my thoughts. For weeks I blamed myself, longing to have one last word with him.

Months after his death, I was still feeling guilty for not adhering to the voice. One night I dreamt my husband and I took a trip. In the dream, my husband and I arrived after dark at this historic looking two story house. We unlocked the front door and took the stairs with our suitcases in hand. Upon passing the first bedroom on the left I noticed the door slightly ajar and a light was on. My husband continued walking down the hall to the last bedroom on the right with our luggage.

Being curious, I stopped in front of the first bedroom. Slowly, I pushed the door open and there stood my grandfather waiting

for me. His body faced the bed, but as I stepped into the room he turned his head in my direction. He looked to be about 30 years of age. His white hair was now salt and pepper, with a stray lock of hair resting on his forward. He was much thinner and stood erect.

In the last three years of his life, his gait and statue had become somewhat unsteady. But here, in this room stood the younger version of my grandfather. He flashed me this great smile, and I remember his teeth being so brilliantly white. I was speechless. Composing myself I asked, "Why are you here, you're suppose to be dead?" My remark caused him to grin even larger. We just stood looking at each other for several minutes. All I could think of saying was; "Well, goodnight Granddaddy," and slowly closed the door. I wish we could have had a lengthy conversation, but in life he was a great man of few words.

The next time I dropped by to visit my grandmother, I asked if she had a photo of my grandfather when he was in his thirties. She motioned to an end table in the living room, stating that she thought there was a picture in the drawer of both of them when they were much younger. Sure enough, lying on top of a lifetime of memories was a photo of my grandparents. They looked to be around thirty years of age.

In the photo was the familiar stray lock of hair. His hair was black with streaks of gray, giving his hair the appearance of salt and pepper. As I stood looking at their photo, I thanked him for finding a way to bring me closure. I have no doubt that our deceased loved ones know when we are thinking of them, and they also know when we could use a visit from them.

Afternoon Tea

On my first night in Charleston, South Carolina, on June 1, 2012, I dreamt of shopping in a gift shop. As I walked around a display table in order to view items on the adjacent table, there stood my best friend Rosemary. She looked to be about 30 years of age. Her face and teeth were glowing and her golden hair fell in short layers away from her face. Rosemary looked so beautiful. In the dream I had exclaimed; "Rosemary, you're here!" Instead of replying she had given me this big brilliant smile. It was then that I woke up. Lately, I had been missing Rosemary, and thinking about how lonely life will be without her. Rosie (my nickname for her) had been my traveling companion. She passed away in March of 2012 due to appendix cancer

We had celebrated my birthday in January at the O. Henry Hotel in Greensboro, North Carolina. We often met there to have afternoon tea and catch up on things. Rosie had been one of those friends that would share spontaneous adventures with me. We took several Amtrak trips, one to Washington to view Jackie Kennedy Onassis's collection of clothes and accessories, another to Raleigh to view the "Titanic" exhibit, and later "The Holocaust" exhibit.

The following afternoon I toured the Charleston Tea House. Here I learned that it was the only tea plantation in the United States. The original owner had discovered tea plants in Summerville (known as the Pinehurst Plantation), that had grown into large trees. He learned with a little research that these plants had been brought over from China in 1880. The Bigelos purchased land from the Lipton Tea Company in 1987 and began producing their own American Classic Tea.

After tasting hot and cold teas I rounded a table and it was then that the dream came back to me. Here I was in a gift shop, and not just any shop, but one that had tea tastings and sold tea. I had even rounded one table to view another one, just like in my dream. There were also all the tea accessories to go along with serving English tea. How appropriate that Rosemary had chosen the night before to come to me in a dream. She must have known that I had made plans to go the week before. No doubt, she would have loved to visit such a place. Maybe she was the one who planted the thought in my mind to tour the tea plantation, and even accompanied me without my knowing it.

A Special Bond

Aunt Claire was from a dying breed. She was what we refer to in the south as a gentile Southern lady. Claire was a caring and loving soul to all who knew her. From the time I was a child we developed a special friendship... a special bond between one another. After I moved away and married we no longer saw each other, but we managed to stay in touch by way of my mother. When Mom came to visit she would bring letters, old photographs, and gifts from Aunt Claire.

In her early seventies, Claire had a severe stroke, leaving her left side paralyzed. Each day, my mother and her younger sister Chris would take turns caring for their sister. On Claire's last day my mother and Aunt Chris sat together by her bedside. They later shared with one another, that they had felt the presence of angels throughout Aunt Claire's house that day.

Right after my aunt passed away I became concerned over some heart problems that I was experiencing. With each passing day my fears mounted. One night in a dream, I looked up to see Aunt Claire sitting on a sofa, floating in front of me. I remember thinking how much younger she looked. She slowly reached down and placed her hands on either side of my face. I could feel how warm and delicate her hands were. With her hands touching both sides of my face, she looked into my eyes and said; "Honey, everything is going to be alright." As she floated off to my right, her hands went right through my face.

I'm happy to relate that after cardio-ablation my heart is now in rhythm. However, ten years later, due to not being able to take Coumadin and being misdiagnosed, more stokes occurred. Today, I'm a living miracle. Although, I use a walker, wear

Depends, and must have sitters with me at all times, I still have my mind.

Author's note:

The concept of deceased loved ones paying us a visit, or giving us messages within our dreams seem to some impossible to believe. Instead, we allow doubt to slip in. Many will reason that having such an experience was merely a dream like any other night. In fact, this was more than a dream. This was a visitation from the other side... this was a message that Sam needed to hear at that time in his life. The special bond that his aunt and he shared in life could not be broken, even in death. Claire had found a way to reach through the veil that divides us from heaven and earth, bringing a message of hope to her favorite nephew.

Carol's Closure

After my husband died, I had a hard time accepting his death. At thirty-two years of age, he was far too young to die from a fatal heart attack. The thought that I could have done something more to save his life played over and over in my mind. After all, I had saved him once before by performing CPR.

Several months passed, before Tim appeared to me in a dream. I had just drifted off to sleep, and in my dream I looked up to see my deceased husband smiling down at me. As Tim floated over my bed he telepathically said, "Don't grieve anymore, you did all that you could." I reached out for him and begged him not to leave, but he floated up through the ceiling and was gone.

Within that same week, my daughter Erin dreamt she was walking in a meadow full of vibrant flowers, when suddenly she felt her father's arm around her waist. They continued to walk together through the meadow side by side. Erin told me that she turned to face him and said, "Daddy, please stay with me." He replied, "I can't, I'm where I should be." She stated that when he turned to go he began to float upwards. Erin reached for him and he extended his hand saying, "Be happy, it will be alright. I'm where I ought to be."

Author's note:

It appears that our deceased loved ones are aware of our distress on this side. At times spirits choose to pay us a visit when they see that we're not able to move forward due to our grief or our feelings of guilt.

Visions come to some with eyes wide open, while others experience visions with eyes closed. It is similar to watching a movie. You may see the ceiling, or a wall opening up to another dimen-

sion. You may be viewing a beautiful scenic landscape, or an enactment-taking place. Visions may include a loved one, or even a deceased pet. With each experience the deceased one appears to recognize you. Some foretell future events, while others allow you to visit with ones from the other side.

My Grandmother's Pendant

Early one morning my mother called, stating that my grandmother had passed away. Upon hanging up, I chose to sit in my den, reminiscing of the good times we had shared together. Suddenly, I'm twelve years old and I'm in the Fifty-Fifty Store, my grandmother is buying me a double scoop of peach ice cream and a Modern Romance magazine. The magazine was our secret. Now we're walking to her house, carrying the ingredients to make my favorite dessert, chocolate meringue pie. It was her tradition to make two, and it was my job to lick the beaters once the pies were placed in the hot oven.

Twin weeping willows once graced her backyard, and many a weekend was spent in my younger years swinging on their vine-like branches, pretending to be Jane out of an episode of Tarzan. As a youngster, many Saturday nights were spent in her bed sharing ghost stories. One night the old bed slats gave way and we ended up on the cold linoleum floor. At first, I was frightened, but within minutes she had me laughing at how awkward we looked sprawled out on the floor.

My grandmother lived in an impoverished section of town on Foy Avenue. I would often exclaim that one day I would buy her a grand house. Her home backed up to the railroad tracks, and long after she had fallen asleep, I would lie awake listening for the train to pass by on its way to unknown places. The eerie sounds of creaking boards could be heard, as cars drove over the old wooden bridge that covered the tracks behind her house. To this day, thoughts of her float back to me when I hear a lone train whistle.

There she sits in her favorite overstuffed chair, reading a well-worn Bible, with her priceless almanac by her side. My grandmother religiously lived by both books. Over the years I've kept one of her almanacs, dated 1968. Her last Christmas card, addressed to me is displayed each year among the many cards sent from family and friends during the holiday season.

My grandmother crossed over when I was in my mid-twenties. The week before her death that inner voice had encouraged me to visit. Unfortunately for me, having waited until the next week, I was too late. It was then that I asked for a sign that my grandmother had forgiven me for not taking the time to see her more often.

Having closed my eyes, I found myself viewing a mother-of-pearl pendant with a violet flower in the center. Within the vibrant petals sat a brilliant amethyst. Was this my sign, and if so what did it mean? A heavy sleep soon invaded my questioning thoughts.

At the funeral home I managed to gain enough courage to view my grandmother for the last time. As I took one last look, there was the pendant that had been in my vision. It hung on a delicate gold chain, fastened around her neck. Suddenly, I remembered seeing it among her trinkets one day as she showed me the contents of her jewelry box. She had indicated that it had belonged to her oldest daughter Daisy, who had died at the age of eighteen. The amethyst had represented not only Daisy's birthstone, but my grandmother's as well. My answer had come by way of a forgotten piece of jewelry. After sharing this story with my mother, she later gave me my grandmother's beloved pendant.

Several times a year I take the time to drive by my grandmother's old house. Repairs have been made to the sagging porch, and vinyl has been replaced with batten board siding. The Weeping Willows in the backyard have long been cut down along with the twin Mulberry trees that once shaded the front lawn. The rusty iron fence that once stood guard has left its post, and the squeaky gate no longer swings open to welcome a little girl with pigtails to come in and play. The only detail that time has not erased is the style of the aging house. All appears to be lost, but everything remains unchanged within the archives of my mind.

Author's note:

This story won fourth place in a writing contest put on by Xulon Publishers, the publisher of this book. Had I not prayed for a publisher to be placed in my path, I'm not sure if this book would have ever been printed. I happened to open my e-mails one day, only to stumble upon a writing contest that Xulon was putting on. I was torn between submitting this story or another one. However, after asking my friends, and with much thought, I chose this one to enter. It was a season in my young life that holds so many wonderful memories for me, a time that is close to my heart. Out of over 500 entries, my story placed in the top five. The number five has always been my lucky number.

At the time this was written, I had not acknowledged that the spiritual side was exactly speaking to me by way of that soft inner voice. I thought it was merely my imagination each time. In fact, through the years, not only had I missed seeing my grandmother one more time, but also a dear friend, and my grandfather. Now when I feel a sense of urgency to go see certain individuals, or they remain on my mind, I make it a point to listen to that voice from within.

Betty's Vision

My youngest son, Randy, was only twenty-one when his car ran off the road, killing him instantly. He had been having car trouble and had driven over to his older brother's garage to work on it. They had finished up a little after eleven and Randy was driving home when he had his fatal accident. At the time, I was a nurse and was working the night shift when I received the news. Like many other mothers, I had a hard time accepting his death.

Six months passed by before I had a vision. I had arrived home one morning after working a full shift. While sitting on the edge of my bed I asked God why this had to happen. Instantly, another dimension opened up and there were white clouds floating in a vivid blue sky. My son was sitting on the other side of a stream, smiling at me. He was not solid; he was in a spirit form. He said, "Mamma, don't grieve for me, I'm happy." Then the vision disappeared. I was so happy that I was able to see my son one last time. Not only did it bring me peace, it brought me closure.

Major's Untimely Leap

After finishing my housework late one night, I went to bed at one o'clock. Closing my eyes, I had a vision. I saw one of our horses lying down in a dark enclosed space. The horse appeared to be dead. It frightened me so, that I jumped out of bed and ran outside to check on our horses. Bo was grazing quietly in the front pasture, while Major was standing in his stall. When I came back to the house my husband asked if I was o.k., and I shared what had been shown to me.

Three weeks later, I arrived home from work and Sam, my husband, met me at the door looking quite distraught. He asked me to sit down, that he wanted to tell me something. He began to go over what had just transpired. Sam related that, on this particular afternoon, Major was running his usual last lap, when he picked up too much speed rounding the upper pasture. Sam told me that he could tell that the horse was in trouble, because he was not going to be able to brake in time before hitting the fence. Major, our large, red Paso Fino had a habit of taking one last lap around the pasture each day before being taken to the barn.

Major's decision to jump the fence came too late. His massive body came down on the top rail, splitting the fence. The splintered rail impaled him, before he managed to jump off and run into our neighbor's barn. Sam told of finding him lying in one of our neighbor's stalls. Major had severed a major artery. Sam went on to say that he had no choice, but to put him down.

I've often wondered why only the facts were shown to me, and not the event itself. I once thought that had my vision

revealed more; Major's death could have been prevented. I now feel that it was to prepare me for what was to take place, for it was Major's time to cross over.

Epilogue

"You're here not by chance, but by God's choosing. His hand formed you and made you the person you are. He compares you to no one else – you are one of a kind. You lack nothing that his grace can't give you. He has allowed you to be here at this time in history to fulfill his special purpose for this generation."

...Roy Lessin [28.]

Why is it so hard for us to believe in the supernatural? What are we so afraid of, and why do we care what people think if it benefits our well-being? Unfortunately, many of us are not being taught how to tap into God's greatest resources through the Holy Spirit. I've seen the spiritual side of God and it is very real. It is a side that is often overlooked and many times forgotten. It is a side that even the most devout Christian refuses to acknowledge. It is a side that many churches will not invite in due to their own doubts and fears.

I do not think God would leave us here without some guidance or some protection. I believe he wants us to be aware of angels and guardian spirits who do just that. I believe he wants us to know how to protect ourselves from evil spirits. "My people perish for lack of knowledge," he states in the bible. As you begin to study the bible and do your own research, remember to pray for discernment.

Imagine being placed outside a large maze with numerous winding paths... paths that take years to travel. Some of us are not interested in looking for the entrance, while others are not aware that the maze even exists. Then there are those who are

searching for the correct path that will lead them to the center... the center being God.

Since embarking on my journey over fifteen years ago, my views have slowly changed. This book has been a learning experience, for I too have allowed my doubts and fears to cloud my vision. In fact, my early views were quite staunch and conventional within my religious beliefs.

I cannot expect everyone reading these pages will have a life changing experience, or that it will alter the way in which one views the spiritual world. I do know that God placed the desire to write this book within me and due to this, he has provided me with the tools and the people needed to complete it. A minister's wife prophesied, confirmations were made, and the provisions needed were always granted.

I can only hope that a miracle... a healing takes place... that fear will no longer block your path... and that your spirit will soar to greater heights. Our human side has a way of fiercely latching on to a cause... a belief... and not letting go whether it is right or wrong. If the words that lie within these pages made you think, then my mission is complete, for I have planted the seeds.

I do not profess to hold all the answers. I do know that unconditional love and forgiveness is the key, along with helping one another. We are merely passing through to grow more "in spirit." When we take the time to be quiet... to listen... to pray... to fast... to believe, we will often discover what lies beyond what we cannot always see with our physical eyes.

"Keep ascending the mountain of cheerfulness by daily scattering seeds of kindness along the way as best you can, and should mists hide the mountaintop, continue undaunted and you will reach the sun-tipped heights in your own life-experience."

...Anonymous

Author's Afterword

To contact Glenda S. Walters for speaking engagements, or to share your stories, write to or e-mail her at:

Miracles – P.O.Box 239 – Lexington, NC 27293
gswalters@glendawalters.com
www.glendawalters.com

Please include your e-mail address, telephone number, and your return address.

About the Author

Glenda Smith Walters has written numerous articles for DirectPathways, The Dispatch (once owned by the New York Times), and has written her own column for The Thomasville Times. Glenda holds a Diploma in Merchandising from American Business and Fashion, Institute of Charlotte, North Carolina. Throughout her life she has taken writing courses at Salem Academy and College of Winston-Salem, North Carolina. She has been blessed with the best of both worlds. Her prior career dealt with product development within the realm of high-end furniture. While working on location, she worked on a project with Clint Eastwood. After a career that spanned over fifteen years within the furniture industry, Glenda decided to go in another direction... one of service to others.

As an active volunteer with Hospice of Davidson County, she was offered a position as their Volunteer Coordinator. With many of the Hospice patients having spiritual experiences, she decided to record these exciting events. Hospice volunteers, family members, and friends, as well as the author's own experiences, were included within these pages.

While at Hospice, Glenda started a "Lending Library," with the sole purpose of helping the terminally ill overcome their fear of death, along with giving their families a sense of peace. She went on to become the Director of Community Relations and later the Director of Fund Development for Hospice of Davidson County. Her life came full circle through her past contacts within the furniture industry. These same contacts, along with volunteers and the community, aided her in helping to raise funds for

Hospice of Davidson County's new Henry Etta and Bruce Hinkle Hospice House.

She has contracted work through the administrative offices of Old Salem Museums and Gardens, and has held the title of Sales Director for the Lexington Area Chamber of Commerce. She currently works for another Hospice care organization. She continues to write articles on travel and human interest stories in her spare time.

Endnotes

[1] Albert Einstein, Forum and Century, the thirteenth in the Forum Series, Living Philosophies. New York: Simon Schuster, 1931, Ideas and Opinions. New York: Bonanza Books, 1954

Preface

[2] Ari Herzog, Touched by an Angel, Directed by Adam Briles and Ron Brody, PAX-TV, CBS, ION, 1994-2003

[3] Julie Gilfillan and Chris Pechin, It's A Miracle, PAX-TV, CBS, Produced by Weller-Grossman, 1998-2004

[4] Barbara Hall, Joan of Arcadia, CBS, 2003-2005

[5] John Gray, The Ghost Whisperer ABC, CBS, 2005–2010

[6] Mel Gibson and Benedict Fitzgerald, Passion of the Christ, Directed and Produced by Mel Gibson, 2004

[7] Laurie Beth Jones, The Power of Positive Prophecy, Hyperion, 1999, www.lauriebethjones.com

[8] Bonnie McEneaney, Messages, William Morrow, Paperback, 2011

Part One: Blessings and Answered Prayers

[9] Dr. Norman Vincent Peale, minister, author, and publisher of Guideposts, 1945

[10] Adam Sztykiel Writer-Screenwriter, Maid of Honor, Screenwriters Deborah Kaplan, Harry Elfont, Directed by Paul Weiland, The Moving Picture Company, Sony Pictures Releasing, 2008

[11] Cecelia Ahern, P. S. I Love You, Screenplay by Steven Rogers, Directed by Richard LaGravenese, Alcon Entertainment,

Grosvenor Park, 2S Films, Distributed by Warner Bros. Pictures, 2007

[12] Reverend Shell Ministries

Part Two: Between Two Worlds

[13] Henry Van Dyke, Gone from My Sight, a 19th Century clergyman, educator, poet, and religious writer

[14] Barbara Karnes, Gone from My Sight, reprinted, 1986, www. Barbara Karnes.com

[15] Rebecca Springer, Within the Gates, Christ for the Nations, 1990

[16] Dennis and Nolene Prince, interpretation of Marietta Davis's Nine Days in Heaven, Charisma House, 2011

[17] Carol Zaleski, Otherworld Journeys, Oxford University Press, USA, 1988

[18] Black Holes Winston-Salem Journal, Winston-Salem, NC, Jan. 14, 1997

[19] Mary K. Baxter, A Divine Revelation of Hell, Pennsylvania: Whitaker House, 1993

[20] Bruce Joel Rubin, Ghost, Directed by Jerry Zucker, Paramount Pictures, 1990

Part Three: Ministering Spirits

[21] G. Scott Sparrow, I Am with You Always, Bantam Dell Publishing, Westminister, MD, USA, 1995, 1996

Part Four: Angels of the Earth and Air

[22] AP-GfK Poll, 2011

[23] Agatha Christie, Hercule Poirot's Casebook, 1st Ed., GP Putnam, hardcover, 1989

[24] Julie Campbell, Trixie Belden, Original series1948-1986

[25] Carolyn Keene, Nancy Drew, Original series 1930-1956

[26] This Strange Universe, April '97. Created by Paul Barrosse, Produced by Rusher Entertainment, Burbank, California, 1996-1997.

[27] Channel 8 Fox News (WGHP).

Epilogue:

[28] Roy Lessin, Daysprings

ORDER FORM

Send request to:	Return Shipping
G. Walters	Name:
P.O. Box 239	Address:
Lexington, NC 27293	City:
	State/Zip:

Select parables desired	Price	Qty	Total
Life's Many Plays (8.5 X 11)	$19.95		
Life's Many Plays (11 X 17)	$23.95		
This Place That I Go (8.5 X 11)	$19.95		
This Place That I Go (11 X 17)	$23.95		
I Am the Deep Blue Ocean (11X17 only)	$23.95		
	Total Money Enclosed		

Parables are printed on a color photo backdrop, and may be viewed and ordered online at: www.glendawalters.com